THE LIBRARIAN'S CD-ROM HANDBOOK

Supplements to
Optical Information Systems

1. Essential Guide to Interactive Videodisc Hardware
   and Applications
   by Charles R. Miller, III
   ISBN 0-88736-091-2

2. Authoring Systems: A Guide for Interactive
   Videodisc Authors
   by Peter Crowell
   ISBN 0-88736-084-X

3. CD-ROM Applications and Markets
   edited by Judith Paris Roth
   ISBN 0-88736-332-6

4. The Librarian's CD-ROM Handbook
   by Norman Desmarais
   ISBN 0-88736-331-8

THE LIBRARIAN'S CD-ROM HANDBOOK

Norman Desmarais

Meckler

Library of Congress Cataloging-in-Publication Data

Desmarais, Norman.
  The librarian's CD-ROM handbook.

  (Supplement to Optical information systems ; no. 4)
  Bibliography: p.
  Includes index.
  1. Optical disks--Library applications--Handbooks, manuals, etc.
 2. CD-ROM--Handbooks, manuals, etc. 3. Library materials--
Reproduction--Technological innovations--Handbooks, manuals, etc.
I. Title. II. Series: Supplement to Optical information systems ; 4.
Z681.3.067D47   1989   025.17'9   88-9181
ISBN 0-88736-331-8 (alk. paper)

British Library Cataloguing in Publication Data

Desmarais, Norman
  The librarian's CD-ROM handbook.
  1. Libraries. Applications of computer systems.
  Read only memory : Compact discs
  I. Title
  025' .0028'5456

  ISBN 0-88736-331-8

Copyright © 1989 Meckler Corporation. All rights reserved. No part of
this publication may be reproduced in any form by any means without
prior permission in writing from the publisher, except by a reviewer who
may quote brief passages in review.

Meckler Corporation, 11 Ferry Lane West, Westport, CT 06880.
Meckler Ltd., Grosvenor Gardens House, Grosvenor Gardens,
London SW1W 0BS, U.K.

Printed on acid free paper.
Printed and bound in the United States of America.

*To Barbara and our daughters,
Jeanne and Denise*

CONTENTS

Introduction	ix
Chapter 1. Selecting a CD-ROM Product	1
Chapter 2. Hardware	25
Chapter 3. Management Issues	47
Chapter 4. Concerns	59
Chapter 5. Library Applications	69
Cataloging	69
Public Access Catalogs	74
Interlibrary Loan	78
Acquisitions	79
Reference Works	83
Indexes and Abstracts	90
Chapter 6. Specialized Applications	103
Business	103
Medicine	115
Law	120
Government	122
Education	125
Science	127
Geographic Applications	130
Miscellaneous	134
Tools	138
Chapter 7. Future Projections	141
Bibliography	145
Index	155

INTRODUCTION

The introduction of CD-ROM in 1985 opened a new horizon for information managers. Although it is only one of several optical information systems (which include videodisc, write once read many (WORM), optical memory card, erasable discs and compact disc—interactive [CD-I]), it is the one which holds the most promise for librarians and publishers. When publishers produce materials, they intend them to have some form of permanency and not to be modified by the user. Likewise, librarians and information managers aim to preserve mankind's intellectual heritage.

The large storage capacity and the read-only nature of the CD-ROM disc make it an ideal medium for information production/management which should benefit both groups greatly. After all, the formats they usually deal with, paper and microform, are essentially read-only also. The importance of these optical information systems is borne out by their popularity. In the three years since their initial appearance, there have been a large number of products to come on the market and a greater market penetration of those already available.

Selecting and implementing a CD-ROM-based information system offers many new and exciting opportunities for librarians and information managers. It also presents some challenges which may dissuade some from adopting this new medium. This book intends to de-mystify the experience by discussing the various steps from the selection process right through implementation and evaluation.

Although the decision to adopt CD-ROM presupposes prior selection of a product, we will look at some characteristics to consider in making such a decision. We will also look at the hardware configurations and discuss some of the management issues and concerns related to operating a disc-based information system. We will also discuss many applications currently on the market or in development to see what we can expect from such products.

As a bare minimum, users need to have a microcomputer, a disc reader, a means to interface the two, and software to run the system as well as the CD-ROM disc.

CHAPTER 1
SELECTING A CD-ROM PRODUCT

As with the selection of any computer application, the decision regarding purpose and system usage should take precedence over the choice of hardware. In the area of CD-ROM, this means that purchasers should make decisions based on the information content of the disc rather than on the delivery medium. Otherwise, they could get caught up in the technology and lose sight of the purpose for adopting it.

Selection criteria generally follow the same guidelines as those for traditional sources: who are the users, what are their needs, how will they use the system, what are the budgetary constraints, etc. (The user issues will be discusssed in Chapter 3). Some issues particularly germane to CD-ROM selection/evaluation involve the contents, scope, and currency of the database, the retrieval software and indexing, the types of user interfaces, data access time, costs and cost-effectiveness, and standardization.

Database Contents

Potential purchasers need to weigh a variety of factors prior to selecting optical disk products. First of all they must determine their need for a particular database, whether it exists and in what format, and whether its contents meet their requirements. Purchasers should consider the contents of the database(s) and the quality of the data replicated there. They should also determine the scope of the database in terms of subject matter and time-span coverage. Furthermore, a potential purchaser should consider their target audience, its educational level, and its degree of sophistication.

If the product represents the CD-ROM version of another product, one should determine if it is in fact a complete and accurate version of the original. Which edition? Does it include the illustrations? How good are the indexes? The standards for evaluating traditional media still apply here.

Some users assume a tool is comprehensive in scope and may have false expectations of the subject contents. These assumptions affect a user's ability to retrieve suitable information. Modern technologies give us the ability to copy almost anything and everything. Judgment in deciding what to copy and why we need to copy it becomes critical.

Some analysts believe that this phenomenon seems to encourage little or no judgment on the user's part in the selection or use of the information provided. They think that users are not learning to evaluate what is pertinent information. One university librarian decided not to subscribe to InfoTrac because she did not want students to do all their research in *Good Housekeeping*.

It seems users become dependent on optical systems because of their speed and relative ease of gathering large amounts of data. Some reports indicate that some even postpone their search if they cannot get immediate access or if the system is down or otherwise occupied. These users seem to forget that alternative sources exist or they refuse to use them.

Relevancy and Scope of Search

A more important issue which has not been discussed in the literature is how to ensure that the results of a search are relevant and intelligible to the user. Few people are aware of the contents and the scope of the materials they search. Many seem to believe that doing a search on an automated knowledge base provides exhaustive coverage. Without adequate instruction or preparation, someone may search ERIC and think he or she is searching *Readers' Guide to Periodical Literature*. Patrons often don't ask for assistance until they receive incomprehensible results from their search. What about all those who don't realize that they did not search *Readers' Guide* or who only searched the current year of a knowledge base instead of the historical file?

Many large databases exceed the capacity of a single CD-ROM disc; therefore, publishers must address important content decisions which affect buyers. Should they produce the entire database on multiple discs or only segments on a single one? If they opt for the latter, should they segment the data chronologically or by subject matter? Either decision will annoy some buyers. Chronological segmentation has proven more successful because it provides the complete coverage of a database even if only for a limited time span.[1]

The selection of CD-ROM applications will have an effect on the library's collection development policies and decisions. Will an institution acquire all the laserbases in a given area or those that perform related tasks? Will it subscribe to only those for patron use or only those for staff use?

One will need to determine the impact on the collections also. If one decides to cancel print subscriptions to indexes or information sources, he or she will need to consider the potential impact of the consequences of such an action.

On one hand, there may be unnecessary duplication and expense in having both an optical and traditional source. Yet, the added convenience may justify the higher cost. On the other hand, products which have license agreements may require that you return discs upon cancellation of a subscription, leaving the library with no backfiles. In such a situation, the librarian will need to determine whether or not to maintain backfiles of valuable data and how to maintain them.

Some laserbases (such as online databases) introduce a certain degree of frustration when they provide references to information not found in the library. This, in turn, increases the demand for interlibrary loans. Some librarians may want to include in their specifications the facility to match citations against the library's holdings to reduce this frustration and demand on interlibrary loan. Some systems provide seamless interfaces so the user can search both the CD-ROM and the microcomputer's hard disk in a totally transparent manner, i.e., they need not recognize the source of the information.

Retrieval Software and Indexing

Search software may come on the CD-ROM disc itself or on a separate floppy disk. As with any computer program, the search software should be easy to learn, easy to use, and powerful. The CD-ROM environment usually custom-fits the software to the disc's index and information files. This means that the user accepts the search software that comes with the disc and cannot change it if he or she does not like some of the features. Changing software requires selecting another information vendor.

A crucial element in the management of any large quantity of data is its arrangement, classification, or indexing. As the search and retrieval process to access this information depends entirely on the indexing, it must have enough flexibility to satisfy the various user needs and allow different users to retrieve material regardless of their assumptions and terminology.

The process should let the operator use natural language or provide alternatives to avoid any difficulty in identifying the correct search terms or subject headings to use in executing a search strategy. It should also provide tools to reduce large quantities of retrieved information or to increase small amounts. Producers then have a tough challenge to develop software simple enough for the novice to use yet complex enough to perform sophisticated searches.

Quality of the Software

The database should have efficient methods of accessing stored data. The quality of the indexing and search-and-retrieval software will have a great impact on the value of an optical disk. A user looking for a needle in a haystack wants to find the needle, not the haystack.

Besides having the features and characteristics just described, the CD-ROM product should also have file structures suitable to the strengths and weaknesses of the medium. The amount of indexing overhead and the amount of disc space reserved for it determine a database's flexibility and how thoroughly it can respond to user requirements. This in turn determines the process of retrieving information from the disc.

The inverted indexing features used in CD-ROM permit retrieval of any significant word or combination of words. Some CD-ROM manufacturers may not avail themselves of this capability or may use the space for other purposes. To retrieve information, it takes a little longer to position the optical head in the proper location (latency time) than it does for a magnetic head because instead of moving just the head, the drive must move the entire sled that includes the head and tracking device. However, once in position, the optical head scoops up one megabyte (MB) of data in the same time that a magnetic head retrieves a mere 16 kilobytes (KB).

Discs which include data in various formats (audio, text, graphics, etc.) present particular indexing problems. Consider the case of a portion of text which requires simultaneous audio. The disc does not intermingle both types of data; but it must retrieve them simultaneously. One method of indexing in such a case would "interleave" the data in a checkerboard pattern with one block of text followed by one of audio followed, in turn, by another block of text and so on.

Efficient, Effective Access Software

Buyers will want user-friendly, efficient, and effective access software. While reviews of optical products are beginning to increase, buyers will find them mainly in specialized journals dealing with CD-ROM or optical information systems such as *CD-ROM Librarian, Optical Information Systems,* or *CD-ROM Review.* Very few of them have appeared in traditional library reviewing media to guide consumers in evaluating CD-ROM products.

Another aspect of user-friendliness deals more with the manufacturer's quality control. The quality of a database and the resulting searches will suffer if the database contains spelling errors that effectively overlook relevant citations or produce false drops. The relatively narrow "window" that the computer screen offers relative to paper and microform products magnifies the effect of such an error. A misspelled heading or subheading may appear several screens away from its proper location, making it unlikely that a user would discover it by chance.

While one may not find orphan "see" references as often in a CD-ROM product as in traditional tools, they may still exist. Such references appear under one name or heading and refer to another name or heading. When the user looks under the referred heading there is nothing there.

On the other hand, one does not want to multiply steps to retrieve relevant information by having to look under a variety of headings. One strength of an automated retrieval system is the ability to link such headings in a totally transparent manner. Yet, few systems have authority control features to standardize or link variant name forms. As a result, the user must take several steps to locate information. This increases the occurrence of "oversights." For example, one CD-ROM disc includes no less than four forms of Nancy Melin Nelson's name: Nancy Melin, Nancy Jean Melin, Nancy Melin Nelson, and Nancy Nelson. The producer could compound the problem by also including the use of initials.

The software should also have some ability to minimize the number of "false drops." For example, a user searching for information about Alexander Pope (or Pope, Alexander) does not want citations about the pope who resides in Vatican City. The user also needs to beware orphan error messages such as "search too long" that leave the user guessing as to what to do next.

Menu-Driven versus Command-Driven Systems

Buyers will also need to determine whether they want command-driven systems or menu-driven ones. Menus accommodate the novice user but present difficulties to the experienced searcher. On the other hand, the command mode produces more error messages due to syntax errors. The National Information Standards Organization (NISO) has a standard in draft form (Z39.58—198X) which attempts to move toward a common command language for online (and ondisc) information retrieval.

This should minimize the confusion caused by the multiplicity of commands to execute the same step in various databases. It should also bring some standardization to the use of punctuation to identify the various parts of a search such as the beginning or end or limitation to a specific field. Hopefully, it will also address the issue of various truncation symbols and wild card characters.

Boolean Operators

The search software should also provide shortcuts for experienced searchers. These include the ability to interrupt processing and abandon the search or to save it and resume from the cut-off point. Some databases may require powerful software capable of accommodating Boolean operators (AND, OR, NOT), proximity operators, keyword searches, truncation (right or left), command stacking, nesting, cascading, or exploding terms to include related concepts.

If the software provides such sophisticated features, it will also need to accommodate alternate access modes for the novice user. It may also require a variety of display and print capabilities (partial screen, full screen, or save to disk).

Online Tutorials

People generally don't want to read manuals. They prefer to get immediate gratification with hands-on experience. CD-ROM would do well to include tutorials to show where to find certain features, how to use the system, and how to correct errors. It should also provide clear command meanings and error messages as well as explain the subject, scope, and time period covered by the database on the introductory screen to minimize a number of false assumptions in approaching the system.

Documentation

While the casual user may begin searching the CD-ROM discs without referring to any printed documentation, the purchaser should examine all documentation closely while evaluating different products. It often holds the key to efficient use of an application by describing the product's contents and source materials, by explaining the arrangement of files, by offering troubleshooting tips, and suggesting user shortcuts. It will undoubtedly serve as a reference manual to solve any problems with the system or to explain questions regarding peculiarities which may suddenly occur.

The user should also determine whether there is a help line to call in case of any problems and whether or not the documentation makes note of this. This will demonstrate the importance of documentation if users do not understand how to interact with a particular product or if it does not work the way it should.

The printed documentation will often serve only as a reference manual. The user will more often rely on ondisc tutorials and context-sensitive help messages. The purchaser should also seriously consider these forms of documentation in the evaluation.

Customer Support

Customer support from the supplier can present a crucial element to decision making. One should ascertain what services and aids the dealer/producer will provide and at what cost. This includes the amount and quality of the documentation, the availability of a help line, the handling of updates, and the training, if any, required to operate the systems effectively. Advice from clients who tested the products or purchased them may provide valuable insights in this regard.

In addition to the printed documentation, producers can provide support for their products on the disc itself, in an online environment, by field representatives, or at the company's headquarters. We can think of support as an insurance policy. We never know if it's really there or any good until we need it. Consequently the user should establish what kind of support the company provides or promises. He or she should also determine the strength and the stability of the company because if it goes out of business in a year or leaves the CD-ROM business, the user will have *no* support.

Interfaces

Computer peripherals require three types of interfaces:

1. The *hardware interface* which links the various pieces of hardware and permits them to "talk" to each other. It usually consists of a printed circuit board (also called a controller card) that attaches a particular peripheral device to a microcomputer.
2. The *hardware–software interface* which converts system data during input and output to a peripheral device to effect communications between the system and the peripheral. It controls the operation of the programs and instructs the computer on how to handle the various instructions.
3. The *user interface* which converts operator input to machine code and vice versa to produce humanly readable results. It provides the means for the user to learn what the disc contains, to find and retrieve desired data, and to manage whatever he or she needs to do to process it.

The user interface determines what the operator sees on the screen and how he or she processes the displayed data. It consists of menus, commands, displays, etc. as well as the activities or processes for working with the data. There are no standard CD-ROM user interfaces and probably never will be. There is an immense variety of forms to store information on a disc and a wide range of sophistication levels that a product must accommodate. The first two interfaces are discussed in Chapter 2. In this chapter we concern ourselves with the user interface.

Types of User Interfaces

Many CD-ROM products represent an optical counterpart to a corresponding online version from which they migrated. We should not be surprised that the user interfaces resemble those from the computer and online environments. However, the massive amount of data that the CD-ROM stores requires new and different ways of accessing that data to suit individual needs. People have three ways of gathering information—grazing, browsing, and hunting.

Grazing implies passive and aimless reception of data. The eye/mind absorbs whatever it comes across. Typical examples include watching television or a movie and listening to the radio.

Browsing denotes searching a large quantity of data with no explicit target in mind. It implies gathering general information or forming an overall view of a body of data. It also indicates the ability to move to a particular place in a database, display the data, and move to new data. Examples of browsing include skimming a document, reading here and there in a newspaper, scrolling through an electronic document, channel checking on television, or looking around in a department store or library.

Hunting looks for specific bits of information for a well-defined purpose and often requires tools to refine search strategies. Computers fulfill this need superbly through their abilities to locate keywords or to find bits of data in predetermined fields by "querying" or "filtering" data according to a set of user-defined criteria.

While traditional user interfaces familiar to computer users may perform adequately with relatively small amounts of data, they may be incapable of exploiting the potential of the massive amounts of data that CD-ROMs present. As an example of this, try using the PgDn key to quickly scroll through a megabyte of text or a spreadsheet. The user will look for ways to move freely and quickly through large quantities of data while being aware of the context and structure of that data.

Information Hierarchies

Printed materials provide readers with information arranged in a hierarchy to provide an easy overview of the structure and the extent of the information contained there. This permits quick and easy navigation to topic locations. Electronic media provide more fluid hierarchies or outlines.

The small size of the computer screen (lines of text per page) and its resolution (dots per inch) both limit the view of the document and also make it a little more difficult to get a quick overview of the topic. At the same time, the computer often lets the user interact with the electronic outline, to expand or reduce it to display the desired level of detail. It also lets the user channel commands to the lower levels of an electronic outline by selecting the appropriate heading and issuing the command (such as Move, Copy, Delete, and Print).

Menus, Trees, and Boxes

Other options to represent information hierarchies include nesting menus (each menu item leads to a submenu), vertical or horizontal trees (organization charts), and nesting boxes in addition to outlines. Each of these methods has its own particular advantages.

An interface dealing with the large quantities of data on the CD-ROM should provide a choice of methods that the user can easily move between. The CD-ROM should allow infinite connections between subjects to allow a user to discover new linkages between topics, a concept known as "hypertext."

While keyword searching offers computer users a powerful tool, it does have its limitations. Often the context of the information is as important as the information itself. Pure keyword access gets users to a fact; but they often cannot remember how they got there or cannot understand the greater context of the fact.

This may cause them to go in loops, wandering down information trails without knowing how the various pieces relate to each other. Hierarchies display the context and the structure and the interrelationships of information as well as lead the user to an individual topic.

Keyword searching provides an excellent method for "unstructured browsing," finding an unexpected connection. Information hierarchies present good means for "structured browsing," exploring specific subject areas while maintaining an orientation to the information and keeping it in perspective. Both methods are excellent for hunting or zeroing in on specific information as rapidly as possible.

Hierarchies could serve to move up and down the various levels of detail in a CD-ROM's information. They could also make keyword links continuously available for making "sideways" jumps to any related information.

As a user tries refining the search to locate specific information, he or she must often execute a series of requests to refine a search strategy. Each request modifies and refines the previous one. As the operator evaluates the results of a query against the initial concept, he or she changes it to produce more suitable results. The user interface should facilitate this process as much as possible.

Other elements of the user interface include the use of menus, post-processing including access to online versions of a database, and the ability to print the information, export it to other software packages, or save it to disk.

Menus Benefit Novice Searchers

Most programs present the user with a screen display of choices or paths of action called menus. In addition to making a user aware of what can be done, a menu helps direct the user to select the appropriate action and reminds one how to do it. Each system uses menus in a different way. They accommodate the novice but usually present difficulties to the experienced searcher.

In some cases, the CD-ROM disc may contain the entire database as available online. In other cases, the CD-ROM may contain only subsets of the online version. In either case, the online database will usually include more current or more complete information than its CD-ROM counterpart. Purchasers will want to consider how well a particular application integrates the online and CD-ROM versions.

A purchaser should also recognize that not all interfaces permit executing a search on the disc and automatically repeating it on the online database for the most current information. Those interfaces which offer online access also display a wide range of possibilities. Some applications only permit executing the search on the identical online counterpart while others let the user access all the databases in a particular databank and/or provide gateways to other databanks.

Post-Processing

After locating desired information from the CD-ROM or magnetic tape (online) and viewing it on the screen, the operator usually wants to transfer it to other storage media such as paper or a floppy or hard disk. The operator would like some level of integration among the various applications he or she uses for locating and displaying information and those used for other work (text and graphics processing, spreadsheets, database management, etc.). Unless the application lets the operator save results in some fashion, whether on paper or on disk, this is simply impossible.

Thus, exporting information becomes extremely important. It permits the user to apply specialized tools with more power to analyze and manipulate the information than the user interface can provide. Otherwise, the interface may end up as merely a passive viewing machine with a possible capability of exporting only fragments of information. Since the writeable disk (hard disk or floppy) has only a fraction of the capacity of the CD-ROM, the user interface must have adequate capabilities built in to support direct manipulation of information.

CD-ROM can support post-processing software in at least three ways. It can include the necessary tools on the disc itself, or it can access them from a magnetic disk. It can also provide tools to format the retrieved information in such a way that the user's own software tools can process it. The buyer should determine what software tool support, if any, the product provides.

Restructuring Downloaded Data

Users should also have the capability to do some amount of restructuring of the information, creating for themselves their own access paths. We know that people learn best when they explore information actively.

"Active" implies that the user controls the viewing, digesting, and structuring of the information; so it does not suffice for CD-ROM user interfaces to provide multiple access paths to their information. No matter how many paths the CD-ROM offers, they remain static and unchanging due to the read-only nature of the medium.

The interface should include features to let the user take an active role interacting with the information much as one does in marking up a textbook to personalize what one reads. CD-ROM will let users get the most out of the underlying information when the user interface supports the electronic equivalent of highlighting, underlining, and marginal notes. This requires interfacing the CD-ROM with the computer's writeable storage and applications software like word processors to create personal paths, structures, outlines, and comments for a particular purpose.

Switching CD-ROM to Floppy

The user interface software could easily switch from reading the overlying outline from either the CD-ROM or the hard (or floppy) disk. The user should even have the option of copying the CD-ROM access paths onto the hard disk to personalize them by rearranging the topics and choosing to view the information through either outline overview. This lets the operator impose his or her own outline (or any kind of structuring) on the information. He or she can thus make the information their own by refitting it to their own context and world view and needs.

This is a difficult task to implement; but it provides the ability to work with and reshape the entire mass of information available on the CD-ROM. Exporting it to disk or printing it works only for relatively small pieces of information until we have writeable media that provide similar storage capabilities, economy, and speed as CD-ROM.

As CD-ROM remains a relatively new medium, many of the interfaces have come from the familiar computer and online environments. Future CD-ROMs may be valued and judged for the degree to which they include creative and innovative additional structure and access paths beyond the raw data itself.

Some applications may benefit from graphic presentation of information or multiple windows to view the same data simultaneously in different ways. Others may include sorted lists of indexed terms or support a pointing device such as a mouse to supplement or replace keyboard input. Other options could include the use of various fonts, color, and graphics

Data Access Time

Data access time is another important consideration. Various storage media provide a wide range of seek times, etc. CD-ROM players operate more slowly than hard disk drives because it takes a little longer to move the sled which holds the lens and focusing mechanism. However, after locating a track, it can scoop up 1MB of data in the same time a hard disk retrieves only 16KB.

The customer must determine how fast he or she needs to retrieve the stored information. One also needs to consider the reliability of the companies and the technologies. Will they be able to keep up with production demands? If multi-user systems are selected, one needs to evaluate satisfactory response time.

CD-ROM gets a lot of criticism because of its slow access rate. The optical disk drive operates faster than a floppy drive but slower than a hard disk. After retrieving the data, however, different search and retrieval systems vary in the speed at which they process it for viewing. We should also stress that the speed is often relative to the type of search and to the user's perception.

A search for information on a single company in a business laserbase will produce results in a second or two while a more complicated one that retrieves a hundred companies and ranks or screens them according to a variety of criteria will take several minutes.

The operator, sitting at the workstation, expects the results immediately. Just as a watched pot never seems to boil, an operator can lose patience with the system in the few minutes it takes to sort all the data. He or she usually fails to realize that to retrieve the same information by conventional means would be very time consuming if not impossible. But when we actively search traditional sources, we often have the illusion of "accomplishing" something and fail to realize the amount of time such a search consumes.

Costs

Costs remain a major deterrent to widespread distribution of CD-ROM products. While the costs of gathering, compiling, and editing data remain pretty much the same regardless of the medium of distribution, the production costs of CD-ROM decrease to about one-tenth those of microform.[2] Production costs of microform, in turn, reflect about one-third the cost of print. Yet, the Digital Information Group's survey of fourteen CD-ROM knowledge bases and their printed counterparts found that the list price for the CD-ROM version averaged 176 percent that of the corresponding print product.[3]

We must remember, however, that this survey was undertaken while the market still had relatively few products available. The past year has seen a great influx of new products and ventures with the consequent availability of the same databases from multiple vendors. These laserbases differ primarily in the search and retrieval software they employ and occasionally in the contents of the discs. Such competition has resulted in some dramatic price decreases from a year ago.

Fixed Cost and Powerful Software

Optical media combine the best of the print and online worlds in that they have a fixed cost like print products and powerful search capabilities like online. However, as the price tags on these systems still remain quite high, one must evaluate the costs of purchasing or renting the hardware along with the costs of the subscriptions and periodic updating/replacement of the discs. Optical information systems have made existing pricing strategies obsolete. We can expect to see this reflected in the subscription costs.

While many optical systems represent slightly different versions or subsets of online databases, some specialized products such as census data and maps have also appeared on the market. Producers continue to wrestle with marketing strategies and pricing structures. As they gain more experience in this relatively new industry, we can expect price structures to stabilize.

CD-ROM, Paper, or Microform

Since producers don't want to cannibalize their customer base, a major factor they will consider in pricing optical systems or in continuing traditional formats is the degree to which libraries continue to purchase resources in print or microform. The Library Corporation, for instance, discontinued producing the microfiche version of Any-Book because the CD-ROM version presented a much more efficient and cost-effective way to distribute and access the same information.

Some librarians cannot realistically cancel subscriptions without affecting the level of services they provide. Many will see CD-ROM as a complement to existing programs or as a new service to integrate with printed indexes and online searching. In some settings, the archival qualities may take precedence over other considerations as optical disks are highly indestructible and offer libraries a virtually permanent storage medium.

The initial capital outlay for equipment can represent a sizable purchase. The hardware, however, retains its utility even if the library discontinues its subscription to a particular CD-ROM product. One should keep capital costs of the hardware separate from the purchase/access costs of the information content. It is true, of course, that budgeting structures at many institutions may conflict with this principle and make it more advisable to purchase hardware bundled with a CD-ROM subscription.

Costs Decrease With Use

Whereas online costs increase with use, laserbase costs decrease with use. The generally fixed costs make budgeting easier; but their present relatively high cost, puts CD-ROM out of range for many libraries. One needs to perform a significant amount of searching on a particular product to reach the break-even point compared with online services.

While the cost-per-search on a CD-ROM product decreases with increased volume of use, librarians may find that they can now provide more information to more patrons for a fixed amount of money than ever before. They may also find it possible to extend ondisc searching services to situations and users previously unserved by online services and to access the databases online only for current information.

As usage transfers from paper to disc and produces less reliance on paper sources, however, information providers can see savings in paper and binding costs, shelving, online costs, and increased convenience. Whereas online services require carefully constructed search criteria to diminish costs, laserbase users can browse at leisure.

One should also budget for some increased staff time for instruction and assistance in using the various products as well as for ongoing supply costs to cover paper and ribbons or ink cartridges. Users love to print; so paper and ink costs may represent a major expense. Also, the success of CD-ROM may create a growing need for additional products.

Budgeting for Ongoing Support

Some people might find initial grants or outside funding available to cover start-up costs of equipment and subscriptions. They will then need to budget for ongoing support. This may prove difficult because of the increasing number of laserbases already available or coming on the market in the near future, requiring carefully-made selection decisions.

Other options for funds could draw on equipment budgets for hardware purchases and acquisitions funds—books, serials, periodicals, or a combination of these, depending on the disc's contents—for the CD-ROM discs. Some libraries may find themselves fortunate enough to receive extra funds for special purchases or receive support from Friends of the Library organizations to acquire some or all of the necessary hardware, if not the subscriptions.

When microcomputers first appeared on the market, they carried price tags out of reach for all but the most affluent segments of society. We have seen those prices tumble sharply in recent years to the point that they now become affordable to most of us. At the same time, their power, memory size, and capacity continue to increase prompting one vendor to state that, if this trend continues, computer memory will be practically free in ten years.

Yet, optical systems carry lower price tags than microcomputers did at the same stage of development. If the costs of optical systems decrease at the same rate as microcomputers did—a reasonable assumption—they should become very affordable within a few years.

Subsidize or Pass on Costs?

Librarians may need to reopen a controversial subject and reconsider whether or not they will subsidize searches on this medium or pass on all or part of the costs to the patron. Some users such as information brokers or legal researchers frequently use pass-through billing to charge their clients for services.

The fixed cost of CD-ROM systems may significantly raise the overhead costs for their libraries. For this reason, librarians may want to incorporate some type of charging mechanism or a billing program to keep track of search time and costs to recoup some of their expenses or even make a profit from heavily-used systems.

One opinion holds that libraries should provide information at no cost to the patron regardless of the delivery medium. However, only the most affluent or well-subsidized libraries can afford to provide such services indiscriminately. Even then, they may need to develop clear and detailed policies and procedures outlining the conditions for using more expensive media over less-costly ones.

Another opinion holds that if the library provides the same information through traditional free sources, there should be no objection to charging patrons for the added convenience of searching the optical product. Some installations have connected a vend-card charging system to the optical system to charge for both searches and printouts in order to recover some of their costs. This is similar to methods adopted by many libraries that provide online search services. Others may decide to support free searching and charge for prints to recoup the cost of paper and ink.

A variation of this approach would add a second workstation to supplement a product that the library already provides for free and which is in such demand that patrons must wait in line to use it.

Patrons would then have the option of paying to use the second station rather than waiting for the first.

Cost Effectiveness

Laserbases should represent useful and salable products to make them economically worthwhile. A successful product needs a wide market for initial viability. A market that is too narrow may not prove to be an economically viable one for sustained growth. Consumers need to evaluate the cost-effectiveness of these products compared with existing methods and alternatives.

This requires an analysis of costs, benefits, or user satisfaction for paper-based, microform, online, and optical disk-based systems for satisfactory comparative data. Yet few organizations have compiled such data concerning their present operations. They must also consider the frequency of use a print or online product receives before deciding to replace it with an optical system.

Dollar For Dollar?

On the other hand, a dollar for dollar comparison may not be totally adequate. One must be able to analyze the cost/benefit on the basis of how much useful information the patron receives in relation to the dollar allocation for the hardware and disc subscriptions compared to the saving in staff time.

Also the hardware allocated to the running of a given system could serve a variety of functions. The system manager will need to decide whether to dedicate the workstations to a particular use or to provide a general purpose station with the users selecting the applications they want to run. This will require a certain amount of disc swapping and the concomitant risk of loss or theft. Of all the optical media, CD-ROM is the most cost/efficient per byte stored, even including hardware costs.

Standardization

While product features, ease of use by inexperienced patrons, and price become the important factors in the selection process, librarians want to subscribe to other CD-ROM databases and have them run on the same equipment. Buying products that use the same retrieval software often means purchasing from the same vendor.

Many people find this too restrictive. They want to have the flexibility to integrate products from a variety of suppliers—something that is not always possible due to the level of compliance with any existing standards.

One can play an audio compact disc on any compact disc player with no modifications. Not so with the CD-ROM discs because of the relationships between the CD-ROM drives and the microcomputer's operating system. There are three levels of standardization that affect CD-ROM: the *physical*, the *logical*, and the *application* levels.

Philips and Sony's Standards

Philips and Sony, the original license holders for the compact disc and CD-ROM set down the physical standards in what the industry popularly refers to as the Red Book. These specify such matters as the disc size (diameter, thickness, center hole dimensions), the rotational speed, the recording density, including the layout of tracks, the number of data blocks, their length, and the location of timing and error codes. The Yellow Book further specifies the physical standards to apply to CD-ROM discs and drives.

Logical level standardization deals with the conceptual or local representation of the information on the disc. This covers such matters as volumes, files, records, and other data elements and their organization according to directories, paths, tables, and so forth to make it possible for a computer to access the data.

The High Sierra Group has addressed these issues and submitted a proposal which has become the de facto standard for the logical file format in the United States. They sent it to NISO (National Information Standards Organization) and ECMA (European Computer Manufacturers Association), NISO's European counterpart, and ISO (International Standards Organization).[4] The few minor differences between the U.S. proposal and ISO's standard have been ironed out resulting in the ISO 9660 international standard.

Application level standardization relates to the manner of representation of the information elements (text, sound, pictures, program code, etc.) within the logical and physical conventions. While no standards yet exist on this level, NISO continues to work on a family of standards which would also define a number of application specific data elements and formats. These include publisher information, data preparer information, copyright file, abstract file, and bibliographic file.

Consumers who faced expensive microcomputer purchases several years ago only to find that they had limited selection of applications software and could not interface with other systems hesitate to invest in a new product which may have the same problems. Fortunately, this situation may soon come to an end with the adoption of standards.

Although a standard exists for the mastering of CD-ROM discs, many producers used proprietary software for the arrangement and retrieval of the data as well as for patching the optical product into the computer's operating system. This has resulted both in a limited transportability of CD-ROMs and an increase in the capital costs of hardware for accessing databases from different publishers.

High Sierra: Some Do, Some Don't

CD-ROM products fall into one of two groups: those that meet the High Sierra standard and those that do not. While sound reasons can influence the purchase of CD-ROMs that do not conform to the High Sierra standard, one should only do so knowingly. Discs produced before the High Sierra standard and those that don't follow it often require proprietary software and hardware, i.e., software or hardware delivered or specified by the information provider.

Although the logical standard for volume and file structure does much to bring uniformity to the CD-ROM environment, it does not address application software issues. And while vendors generally support the High Sierra standard, the systems integrator or software house dictate the data file and index layout on the disc. This significantly affects the performance of some applications.

Because no standard index structures exist, "a particular retrieval software package can access only those databases indexed using a predetermined subset of that specific package's indexing capabilities. Software houses regard their index structure as proprietary and as a key means by which they differentiate their product."[5] Standardizing the index structures may produce a degradation in access capabilities and perceived response time.

Standardizing Hardware Interfaces

There are no standard hardware interfaces (see Chap. 2), although the SCSI (small computer systems interface) is gradually becoming the de facto standard. Application developers will need to support the interface's command set because the applications determine user interfaces, retrieval commands, and menus. Even with a greater degree of standardization, some applications that require very high performance will continue to need unique hardware configurations.

As long as compatibility remains an issue, it will have repercussions on purchasing decisions and on the placement of equipment, CD-ROM products, and services in libraries. Different laserbases with different hardware requirements and configurations require librarians to consider whether or not they will provide dedicated workstations for single applications or multi-purpose workstations. This latter decision may require a jukebox configuration (which is not yet available for CD-ROM) with workstations in various locations to allow users to access any disc from various locations in the building. One may also decide to group similar or compatible products for use with the same system configuration.

Since MS-DOS had a 32MB limit on file size, early applications had to find a way around this limitation. Most producers developed proprietary software with so-called DOS patches to allow the operating system to access the CD-ROM disc and work with the large files there. This meant that applications could not migrate to another CD-ROM drive and microcomputer unless the user loaded the special application software into the computer.

Microsoft's CD-ROM Extensions

Microsoft developed the CD-ROM Extensions software which overcomes this limitation and lets the user configure MS-DOS and PC-DOS to treat the CD-ROM drive as any hard drive with a drive letter of one's own choice.

Previously, the operating system required a "device driver" (software that tells the computer how to communicate with an external device) to access the CD-ROM. Each provider supplied its own because no standard one existed. As a result, systems and products from one provider did not work with those from another vendor.

The CD-ROM Extensions permit greater portability of CD-ROM discs as the application software now can go entirely on the CD-ROM. This eliminates the need for a floppy, although some producers may continue to provide some access/search and retrieval software in this manner. The Extensions work with discs which follow the High Sierra/NISO format standards. As some applications still do not follow these standards, they may require proprietary software and a separate device driver. Furthermore, they may not work with the CD-ROM Extensions.

The CD-ROM Extensions require MS-DOS 3.0 or greater for installation. Microsoft does not want to market them directly to the consumer. Rather, it sells them to the drive manufacturers who, then, will include them with their drives. At present, not all manufacturers have agreed to take advantage of Microsoft's offer. Buyers who get their drives from these manufacturers or as part of a bundled package from the disc producer/vendor may not get the extensions if the application does not require it. In fact, many vendors who produce discs in the High Sierra format still put the access and operating software on a separate floppy.

Those who purchased drives before the development of the CD-ROM Extensions or who do not get them with drives will have to purchase them separately. Microsoft suggests Meridian Data, Inc., one of its early customers, as a source. Meridian Data can be contacted at 4450 Capitola Road, Suite 101, Capitola, California 95010; (408) 476-5858. The Extensions should cost about $50. Given their ready availability and comparatively reasonable cost, their absence from the retail package is a minor annoyance.

The CD-ROM Extensions diskette also contains an installation routine which automatically identifies the device drivers and asks the user which ones to install and where to install them. It then asks for the directory to install the Extensions program (MSCDEX.EXE) and modifies the CONFIG.SYS and AUTOEXEC.BAT files accordingly. One performs this activity once, unless one needs to modify the device drivers. Rebooting the systems then permits reading the CD-ROM drive in the same manner as any other drive.

Although discs manufactured according to the High Sierra standards should work on most CD-ROM drives, there still remain problems in that many applications still have their own unique way of communicating with the CD-ROM drive. Many of the information providers do not yet use the CD-ROM Extensions. As a result, while all the applications may run on the same basic hardware, each requires a different configuration of DOS. They may need different types of device drivers or modifications to the CONFIG.SYS or AUTOEXEC.BAT files for individual computers.

People who have some familiarity with computers and file structures may find a way around this obstacle by making relatively minor modifications to eliminate any incompatibilities among certain products. Some products require more extensive expertise to accomplish this; others remain totally incompatible.

Widespread acceptance and use of the CD-ROM Extensions should do away with this problem and make it no more difficult to change from one CD-ROM application to another than to switch from a spreadsheet to a word processor with the added step of swapping discs. In the meantime, librarians may decide to dedicate CD-ROM workstations to certain applications or only to compatible ones.

Notes

1. Pooley, Christopher. (1987). The CD-ROM Marketplace: A Producer's Perspective. *Wilson Library Bulletin* 62:4, 24–26.

2. Murphy, Brower. (1985). Libraries and CD-ROM: A Special Report. *Small Computers in Libraries* 5 (April), 7–10.

3. CD-ROM vs. Hard Copy: Pricing. (1987). *Optical Information Systems Update/Library & Information Center Applications* 2:3, 15.

4. Harris, Patricia. (1988). NISO CD-ROM Standards Update. *CD-ROM Librarian* 3:1 8–9.

5. Gale, J.C. (1987). Organizations Hash Out CD-ROM Standards. Compatibility Issues. *Computerworld* Aug. 24, 67–68.

CHAPTER 2
HARDWARE

The CD-ROM Workstation

CD-ROM drives are simply peripherals for microcomputers. While some CD-ROM application vendors may offer a hardware combination as a bundled package to facilitate sale of their products, many purchasers may get them from a dealer of choice such as a local computer store or a system integrator. The choice of the hardware should depend on the selected software application rather than the opposite. Not all micros accommodate all CD-ROM applications any more than they do all floppy disk software. Furthermore, not all CD-ROM applications support all CD-ROM drives.

Equipment purchases from a local dealer may represent a true cost savings in many cases, especially for those who take advantage of sales, discounts, or quantity-purchase arrangements available through networks or college and university contracts. However, because dealers can bundle their products in a variety of ways, the purchaser needs to specify the kind of equipment he or she wants, the type of monitor and adapter cards, the kinds of ports, any expansion capabilities, and the number of floppy disk drives required.

The buyer has the responsibility for making sure that the equipment includes all the necessary parts such as the controller card and cable, for integrating the hardware and for seeing that it works. Conversely, a vendor who bundles the hardware with an application guarantees that it will work properly.

Such vendors will usually accept responsibility for the hardware and software failure as will occur on occasion. They realize that it is to their advantage to keep the system running. If it fails frequently, the users often do not blame the equipment but rather the application. A wise consumer determines what kind of support a dealer provides prior to purchasing.

Anticipating Future Needs

When selecting a system, one would do well to anticipate the future and not just purchase for the specific application at hand. Users who decide to buy only the bare minimum find that their needs and expectations soon surpass the capabilities of their hardware. Upgrading the system later often proves more expensive than including the added features in the initial package. On the other hand, future price reductions and added features may sometimes minimize that expense.

Most CD-ROM applications currently on the market run on the IBM PC/XT/AT line of microcomputers and compatibles. A few operate on the Apple Macintosh and many others are now under development. Several producers are also working on Apple versions of products originally designed for the IBM environment. We may also soon see CD-ROM discs for the Commodore Amiga.

PS/2 Compatibility

Even though IBM has discontinued marketing its PC/XT/AT line which supports most CD-ROM applications, users need not worry about compatibility with the new PS/2 line of personal computers. Some vendors have already incorporated the new line in their bundled package.

Online Computer Systems has also developed a new line of intelligent CD-ROM controller cards to work with the microchannel bus architecture of the new products. Designed to be independent of vendor hardware, each card will support up to eight CD-ROM drives. A single IBM PC could have as many as four controllers to govern as many as thirty-two drives. That's a total of 17 gigabytes of storage.

In addition, Tom Lopez, vice president of the CD-ROM Division at Microsoft, emphasizes his company's commitment to the development of CD-ROM standards and products. Microsoft produces the system-level software (the disk operating system (DOS) and OS/2) for IBM and compatible microcomputers and is the strongest supporter of compact disc storage of all the major software houses. Thus, its activities are critical to anyone interested in a stable CD-ROM environment. It has already developed the CD-ROM Extensions discussed in Chapter 1.

Lopez also emphasizes that Microsoft will provide "downwardly compatible CD extensions" to the forthcoming OS/2 operating system designed for the new IBM machines and most current-generation machines that use the Intel 80286 and 80386 chips. As the PS/2 Model 30 uses the 8086 chip and will not run OS/2, it remains an exception.

This will guarantee that existing applications in the MS-DOS environment can migrate to OS/2 with the confidence that the operating system will still properly support the CD-ROM drive. These new machines will only require the development of the necessary interface card such as the Online product described previously.

Color or Monochrome Monitor

Most CD-ROM applications support either monochrome or color monitors. As textual material predominates on the CD-ROM market at present, the selection of either monochrome or color monitor does not yet make much of a difference. Because some products use reverse video or color to highlight certain words, they do not always accommodate monochrome monitors very well. Such highlighted or colorized text may appear the same as the rest of the passage on a monochrome system.

Buyers who want to plan for the future may want to opt for the color monitor because we can expect CD-ROM to make increasing use of graphics (e.g., charts, graphs, photos in an encyclopedia, or even motion video). The color graphic adapter card which the color monitor requires will usually suffice to handle such graphics.

However, if an application requires certain equipment to run, such as an EGA or VGA graphics adapter or Hercules card, the software checks to see if the system contains them. If it doesn't, most programs will return to the DOS prompt and not run the particular application. At least one CD-ROM demonstration disc that requires color support will run the text and audio portions (if audio jacks are installed) and display a blank screen if it cannot display the graphics.

Memory Requirements

While a few applications may require as little as 256 kilobytes (K) of random access memory (RAM), most require a minimum of 512K. Many have already moved to the 640K level. As the programs become more powerful, more user-friendly, and provide more flexibility, we can expect requirements for added amounts of memory. We should soon begin to see CD-ROM applications which make use of artificial intelligence, so-called expert systems. Such applications require large amounts of memory and even 640K may not suffice.

The purpose that the system aims to serve will determine, to some extent, the design of the workstation. While the basic system requires the microcomputer and CD-ROM drive, a particular application may need other equipment or peripheral devices such as additional floppy or hard disk drives, a modem, telefax equipment, a printer, a pointer or mouse, a plotter, and so on.

CD-ROM Drives

An essential peripheral for reading the CD-ROM disc is the drive. It usually comes with the appropriate controller card and interface cable. It is not an alternative to magnetic disks because it has no recording facility. Essentially, the CD-ROM drive boils down to a supplemented basic compact disc player that includes a relatively small amount of data path hardware, control hardware, and software which can come in the form of a single computer chip.

As with any product on the market, buyers have a wide selection to choose from. Since the Philips/Sony Yellow Book standard sets down the technical criteria and specifications for CD-ROM, the decision will often revolve around a combination of factors such as price, appearance, and features.

A primary factor to consider in drive selection is whether it is to be an internal or external one. All early CD-ROM drives were external peripherals that sat between the central processing unit (CPU) and the monitor or beside the CPU. Some had top-loading mechanisms while others had front-loading devices. All external drives have a separate power supply requiring an electrical outlet.

The first internal drives came as full-height drives with front-loading capabilities. They occupied a space in the CPU much like hard disk drives. Because they reside in the CPU and operate on that power supply like internal hard disks and modems, they do not require a separate electrical outlet. By mid-1987, half-height drives which plugged into the CPU and occupied half the space previously required began to appear.

Some half-height drives may require a "caddy" to hold the CD-ROM disc. This resembles the jewel box that the disc originally comes in. However, it has a covering mechanism that retracts upon insertion into the drive, thus permitting the laser to read the data. It provides added protection for the disc and keeps it in the proper position when the

CPU (and the drive) rests on its side rather than flat as can be done with the AT.

An internal drive has an advantage in that it can provide a bit more security for the disc—especially if a card describing the product or outlining the meaning of the function keys covers the front of the CPU. This type of configuration usually appears transparent to the user who may think that the information comes from a magnetic disk.

Systems with no card or other covering over the CD-ROM drive can use a locking mechanism to reduce the temptation to tamper with the drive or the disc. Some drive manufacturers, like Philips, have included a locking mechanism on some of its models to prevent unauthorized removal of the disc.

Audio Capabilities as an Option

Some newer model drives come with audio capabilities as a standard feature or as an option. This usually consists of output plugs: one for a headphone and a pair for stereo speakers. These drives will play the increasing number of CD-ROM discs that incorporate audio information such as instructions, music, sound effects, etc. Some may also play digital audio discs while others will just hang up the system upon attempting this. The solution requires rebooting. As they compete for sales, some manufacturers tout quicker access and seek times.

Buying the CD-ROM Drive

CD-ROM drives are still somewhat difficult to buy because few companies sell a single drive to an individual consumer. Most sell them in original equipment manufacturer (OEM) agreements. Applications developers often participate in such agreements and usually bundle the drives as an option with their products. This will soon change as a result of agreements announced at the third Microsoft CD-ROM Conference in March 1988. Tandy Corp. will sell Hitachi drives in its Radio Shack stores and Sears will carry the same drives under the Amdek label and bundled with Microsoft's Bookshelf.

Until then, the easiest approach is to call the publisher/distributor of the CD-ROM disc desired for purchase. Most of them sell or lease drives with the products they market. If they do not have a drive distribution program, they will be able to refer the request to an appropriate dealer.

Companies that will gladly sell only a drive without a product represent the exception rather than the rule because disc producers generally have no desire to become hardware distributors.

The second option requires contacting an OEM dealer or sales representative. This may result in a referral to a local dealer. Some drive manufacturers have no outlet to sell single drives and also want to keep their client list confidential. This makes it impossible to purchase a drive without knowing which companies act as OEMs.

Microsoft Corporation also markets its CD-ROM Extensions through OEM agreements; but not all drive manufacturers and vendors have taken advantage of this program. Consequently, while drive purchasers should receive a copy of the Extensions along with the drive, they may not do so if the supplier does not get them from Microsoft or if the application uses proprietary software which does not correspond to the High Sierra/NISO standard.

Before we look at the available models, let us clarify some terms. We shall deal with the interfaces later in a separate section. However, we should note that *compact disc—audio* (CD-A) indicates that the drive can play CD-ROM discs which include audio portions. The *data transfer rate* means the rate at which one device sends information to another device. The *seek time* refers to the amount of time it takes the CD-ROM drive to locate a sector on the disc. The *access time* describes the amount of time it takes to get a unit of data from the CD-ROM disc to computer memory. *Latency* refers to the rotational delay time from a disc file or the time a digital computer requires to deliver information from its memory.

The following pages describe some of the available CD-ROM drives in detail. They are in alphabetical order by manufacturer's name.

Amdek
1901 Zanker Road
San Jose, CA 95112
(408) 436-8570

Amdek is currently the only retailer to market CD-ROM drives to the end-user. Its Laserdrive 1 consists of a repackaged Hitachi CDR-1503S under the Amdek label. It lists at $999 for the drive alone. However, Amdek has decided to bundle the drive with Microsoft's Bookshelf and CD-ROM Extensions at a suggested retail price of $1,099.

At Microsoft's 1988 CD-ROM Conference, Amdek announced two new drives: the Laserdek 1000 (half-height, built-in) and the Laserdek 2000 (stand-alone, front-loading).

Apple Computer, Inc.
20525 Mariani Avenue
Cupertino, CA 95014
408-996-1010

Model: Apple CD SC

Dimensions: Not available
Type: Stand-alone, front-loading
Interface: SCSI, CD-A
List Price: $1,199

Denon
27 Law Drive
Fairfield, NJ 07006
(201) 575-7810

Model: DRD-550
Dimensions: 5.75" x 3.75" x 8"
Type: Stand-alone or built-in, front-loading
interface: SCSI, CD-A, or custom
List price: OEM pricing

Model: DRD-250
Dimensions: 5.88" x 1.75" x 8"
Type: Built-in, half-height
Interface: IBM/PC/XT/AT
List Price: OEM pricing

Model: DRD-251
Dimensions: 5.88" x 1.75" x 8"
Type: Built-in, half-height
Interface: SCSI
List Price: OEM pricing

Digital Equipment Corp.
2 Mount Royal Ave.
Marlboro, MA 01752
(617) 480-4820

Digital Equipment Corp. also markets the Philips/LMSI, CM100, and CM 110 with different interfaces.

Model RRD50-QA: MicroVax II interface
List Price: $1,200

Model RRD50-EA: VAXmate, IBM/PC/XT/AT interfaces
List Price: $1,200

Model RRD50-AA: for use with two-disc system only
List Price: $1,000

Hitachi
401 West Artesia Boulevard
Compton, CA 90220
(203) 537-8383

Model: CDR-1502S
Dimensions: 17.12" x 3.35" x 11.38"
Type: Stand-alone, front-loading
Interface: IBM/PC/XT/AT, 8-bit parallel
Data Transfer Rate: 176K/sec. (nominal), 153K/sec. (minimum)
Seek Time: 1 msec. (track to track)
Average Latency: 70 msec. (inner), 150 msec. (outer)
Access Time: 1 sec. maximum (0.5 sec. average)
List Price: $899

Model: CDR-2500
Dimensions: 6" x 3^1/$_4$" x 8^3/$_8$"
Type: Built-in, full height
Interface: IBM/PC/XT/AT, 8-bit parallel, CD-A (optional)
Data Transfer Rate: 153K/sec.
Access Time: 1 sec. maximum (0.5 sec. average)
Average Latency: 70 msec. (inner), 150 msec. (outer)
Access Time: 1 sec. maximum (0.5 sec. average)
List Price: $899

Model: CDR-2500S
Dimensions: 6^1/$_8$" x 3^1/$_2$" x 13^1/$_{16}$"
Type: Stand-alone, front-loading, full height
Interface: IBM/PC/XT/AT, 8-bit parallel, CD-A (optional)
Data Transfer Rate: 153K/sec.
Average Latency: 70 msec. (inner), 150 msec. (outer)
Access Time: 1 sec. maximum (0.5 sec. average)
List Price: $899

Model: CDR-1503S

Dimensions: 14^9/$_{16}$" x 3" x 13"
Type: Stand-alone, front-loading
Interface: IBM/PC/XT/AT, CD-A
Data Transfer Rate: 153K/sec.
Seek Time: 1 millisecond (msec.) (track to track)
Average Latency: 70 msec. (inner), 150 msec. (outer)
Access Time: .8 sec. (typical)
List Price: $884

Model: CDR-1553S

Dimensions: Not available
Type: Stand-alone, front-loading
Interface: SCSI, CD-A
List Price: $1,199

Model: CDR-3500
Dimensions: 5.84" x 1.652" x 8.2"
Type: Built-in, half-height
Interface: IBM/PC/XT/AT, SCSI, CD-A
List Price: $869

At the 1988 Microsoft CD-ROM Conference, Tandy Corporation announced that it would begin marketing Hitachi drives and Microsoft's CD-ROM products through its Radio Shack stores.

JVC
41 Slater Drive
Elmwood Park, NJ 07407
(201) 794-3900

Model: XR-R100
Dimensions: 9.06" x 2.75" x 13"
Type: Stand-alone, front-loading
Interface: SCSI
List Price: $1,500

Model: XR-R1001
Dimensions: 5.75" x 1.63" x 8.06"
Type: Built-in, half-height
Interface: SCSI
List Price: $1,000

Panasonic
1 Panasonic Way
Secaucus, NJ 07094
(201) 392-4602

Model: SQ-D1
Dimensions: 5³/4" x 1⁵/8" x 8"
Type: Built-in, half-height
Interface: IBM/PC/XT/AT, SCSI
Data Transfer Rate: 150 K/sec (sequential), 1MB/sec. (maximum)
Access Time: 0.65 sec.
List Price: $1,495: $1,695 with SCSI

Model: SQ-D101
Dimensions: 6¹/16" x 3²⁵/32" x 13³/8"
Type: Stand-alone, front-loading
Interface: IBM/PC/XT/AT, SCSI
Data Transfer Rate: 150K/sec (sequential), 1MB/sec. (maximum)
Access Time: 0.65 sec.
List Price: $1,695; $1,895 with SCSI

Philips/LMSI (Laser Magnetic Storage International)
4425 ArrowsWest Drive
Colorado Springs, CO 80907
(303) 593-4269

Model: CM100
Dimensions: 12.63" x 4.56" x 10.5"
Type: Stand-alone, top-loading
Interface: IBM/PC/XT/AT, Apple IIe
List Price: $1,050

Model: CM110
Dimensions: 12.63" x 4.56" x 10.5"
Type: Stand-alone, top-loading
Interface: SCSI
List Price: $1,350

Model: CM201
Dimensions: 5.75" x 1.63" x 8.13"
Type: Built-in, half-height
Interface: IBM/PC/XT/AT, Apple IIe
List Price: OEM pricing

Model: CM210
Dimensions: 5.75" x 2.25" x 8.13"
Type: Built-in, half-height
Interface: SCSI
List Price: OEM pricing

Reference Technology
5700 Flatiron Parkway
Boulder, CO 80301
(303) 449-4157

Reference Technology offers four drives under its CLASIX 500 series. These include the Hitachi 1502S, Sony CDU-100, CDU-5002, and Philips/LMSI CM100, all priced at $990.

Sanyo
200 Riser Road
Little Ferry, NJ 07643
(201) 440-9300

Model: ROM-2500
Dimensions: 5.75" x 1.63" x 8"
Type: Built-in, half-height
Interface: IBM/PC/XT/AT, SCSI
List Price: OEM pricing

Model: ROM-300
Dimensions: 5.75" x 1.63" x 8"
Type: stand-alone, front-loading
Interface: IBM/PC/XT/AT, SCSI
List Price: OEM pricing

Sony
655 River Oaks Parkway
San Jose, CA 95134
(408) 432-0190

Model: CDU-100
Dimensions: $10^{1}/_{2}$" x $4^{1}/_{4}$" x $8^{3}/_{4}$"
Type: Stand-alone, front-loading
Interface: Sony bus
Data Transfer Rate: 150 K/sec
Average Latency: 66 msec. (inner), 150 msec. (outer)
Access Time: 0.7 sec (average), 1.1 sec. full-stroke, typical
List Price: $690

Model: CDU-5002
Dimensions: $5^{3}/_{4}$" x $3^{1}/_{4}$" x 8"
Type: Built-in, full height
Interface: Sony bus
Data Transfer Rate: 150 K/sec.
Average Latency: 66 msec. (inner), 150 msec. (outer)
Access Time: 0.7 sec (average), 1.1 sec. full-stroke, typical
List Price: $590

Toshiba
9740 Irvine Boulevard
Irvine, CA 96280
(714) 583-3117

Model: XM-2000A
Dimensions: 6" x 3.38" x 13.75"
Type: stand-alone, front-loading
Interface: SCSI, CD-A
List Price: OEM pricing

Model: XM-2000B
Dimensions: 5.75" x 3.25" x 8"
Type: Built-in, full height
Interface: SCSI, CD-A
List Price: OEM pricing

While Toshiba markets only on an OEM basis, LoDown retails the Toshiba XM-2000A for $1,595 for applications running on the Macintosh.

LoDown
10 Victor Square
Suite 600
Scotts Valley, CA 95066
(408) 438-7400

LoDown retails the Toshiba XM-2000A for $1,595 for applications running on the Macintosh.

Drives: The Bottom Line

The Toshiba drive retrieves data the fastest; but it has the highest list price. While the Philips drives perform relatively slowly, they have better error correction devices. This means that the drive can still read a CD-ROM disc even after a considerable amount of abuse. The Sony drives have good speed and good error correction mechanisms as well as a list price comparable to that of the Philips drives.

Hitachi drives perform similarly to the Sonys. However, they generally have a lower list price, with some available for around $600. As we see an increasing number of CD-ROM drives appear in computer stores, we can expect an acceleration in the trend to lower prices. The appearance of horizontal market applications such as Bookshelf will also contribute to increased sales and competition which, in turn, will drive down prices.

The reliability of a CD-ROM drive generally runs between 10,000 to 11,000 hours mean time between failures. That's equivalent to operating it 24 hours a day for 59 to 65 weeks. When a failure occurs, it usually involves the replacement of the laser unit which costs about $100.

Interfaces

The Philips/Sony Yellow Book standard (1980) defines the physical characteristics of CD-ROM discs and drives. It ensures physical compatibility of CD-ROM players and discs and suggests standard data encoding and decoding conventions as well as error-correction schemes. It also standardizes the encoding of specific operational data on the disc such as the laser position and the control servo-mechanism for tracking and focusing. This means that every CD-ROM player—by Hitachi, Sony, Denon, Philips, Panasonic, and others—should play any CD-ROM disc.

Unfortunately, the Yellow Book standard does not provide for standard disc file formats—a critical software concern. Nor does it specify standardized computer/CD-ROM hardware interfaces, software protocols, and file structures among the competing systems. Thus, several drives require special proprietary interface cards for use with a PC.

The industry is currently moving toward two standards. The first is for the hardware—the SCSI interface (pronounced "scuzzy," an acronym for Small Computer Systems Interface). The other is for the hardware–software interfaces—Microsoft Corporation's MS-DOS CD-ROM Extensions.

SCSI

The SCSI interface consists of a standard 8-bit parallel interface frequently used to connect computer disk drives to a microcomputer. It can also run many other peripheral devices. It permits the addition of mass storage, optical storage, local area networks, printers, plotters, modems, and other devices to the microcomputer by providing an easy method of eliminating cost-consuming interfacing tasks and by providing a rich set of commands and a defined bus structure.

SCSI also handles many routine chores without tying up the microcomputer. It also permits the computer to go promptly to the next operation rather than making it wait for the peripheral (CD-ROM drive in this case) to execute the command. It then proceeds to the next task. That is not so for the SASI interface (pronounced "sassy," an acronym for Shugart Associates Standard Interface).

The SCSI interface, which the industry seems to prefer as the CD-ROM-microcomputer connection, permits the CD-ROM drive to work with IBM PCs and compatibles, Apples, or virtually any other micro. This standard will eventually do away with driver-specific interface cards (printed circuit boards) for the PC. For the time being, however, the PC will need a SCSI host adapter because most CD-ROM drives have SCSI controllers built into them. These host adapters will also allow the connection of different drives to one host adapter. SCSI will also standardize all physical connections between any CD-ROM player and any microcomputer.

SCSI as Electronic Translator

SCSI incorporates commands that allow such features as formatting of storage devices; the ability to read and write to and from peripherals; setting special file marks for locating data; directing output to various hard copy attachments or storage devices; or copying the data from one machine to another or sending it to other hosts.

Its purpose is to join mismatched devices electronically so that one device can translate and use the signals from another. In addition to acting as an electronic translator, the SCSI interface defines a complete bus system that clearly determines specific electrical paths and communication protocols.

The existing SCSI controller can support up to eight logical units in any configuration or combination. Examples include one host computer with seven peripherals, seven hosts and one peripheral, or other combinations. Adding a gateway to a local area network (LAN) will permit connecting even more devices.

Alternatively, each of the eight logical units can support an additional seven units, with one device serving as the bus master. Such a fully-loaded system, however, will suffer performance degradation.

The interface's key advantages include its ability to serve a wide range of performance requirements such as multi-user, multi-tasking applications and the capability to control seven peripherals through a single backplane slot. Because SCSI serves as its own "traffic cop" to arbitrate bus access, system integrators need only concern themselves with data management at the point of access to the SCSI bus, the host-computer adapter which provides the vital link between the system bus and SCSI.

Potential purchasers should determine whether or not a given CD-ROM disc will work with a drive interfaced to the micro through SCSI. Some vendors may have good reasons for using either a non-SCSI drive or a disc which cannot operate with a SCSI interface. The buyer should make the choice deliberately.

CD-ROM Extensions

The MS-DOS CD-ROM Extensions allow the disk operating system (MS-DOS or PC-DOS) program to handle data files larger than 32MB, a current DOS limitation). They comprise two software modules: 1) a hardware-independent program and 2) an installable device driver customized by manufacturers to meet the requirements of their hardware.

Microsoft supplies the hardware-independent program (via vendors) along with a sample device driver and documentation. Users may need to modify the drivers on occasion, especially if trying to run several products from different vendors on the same drive. Someday, CD-ROM Extensions may come bundled with the disk operating system.

The Extensions permit systems running MS-DOS 3.1 or higher to access the CD-ROM as if it were a magnetic fixed disk, and provide access to the disc's complete 550MB capacity. As this presupposes that the workstations will know file structure, size, and location, it requires compliance with the High Sierra/NISO standard. The Extensions also allow companies to distribute desktop publishing systems with many fonts, click art, and other enhanced features.

Producer Incompatibility

Buyers should note that the latest version of the Hitachi driver supplied with the CD-ROM Extensions will not function with earlier model Hitachi interface cards (CD-IFI2) or with those designed by Reference Technology, Inc.

CD-ROM drive manufacturers license Extensions from Microsoft and provide an Extensions diskette and a sub-license with the purchase of a drive. While most major manufacturers cooperate in this effort, some suppliers may not provide the Extensions, especially if their applications do not conform to the High Sierra/NISO standard or if they use proprietary device drivers or custom software to access the CD-ROM disc via DOS patches.

In order to increase market acceptability for end-users, system integrators, and original equipment manufacturers, most CD-ROM drive vendors have advocated a plug-and-play design that emphasizes ease of use with personal computers as well as convenience. Until the controller card (printed circuit board) comes built into the CD-ROM drive, it will come with the drive and connecting cable for the user to install in the PC.

Installing the Interface

While a computer novice may deem installing the interface a frightening prospect, it is a relatively simple process that should not cause any concern. It installs just like any other card for computer peripherals such as a printer, modem, mouse, etc. and simply requires removing the casing from the CPU to locate an available expansion slot usually at the rear of the unit. After removing the metal covering, the user takes the controller card and places it on the motherboard, gently pressing it into the slot until all contacts are firm. After screwing the card to the CPU to hold it firmly in place, the user replaces the covering and plugs in the connecting cable.

As all computer peripherals have "idiot plugs" which accept connectors sized solely for the particular application and which only fit one way, it is physically impossible to make an error without forcibly ruining the connection. At least one vendor simplifies this even more by color coding the various connections so the user just has to match the colors. After connecting the cable between the PC and the CD-ROM drive, the user can plug in the power cord, and boot the computer to begin processing.

A first time user will need to install any necessary operating software (such as Microsoft's CD-ROM Extensions or vendor-supplied applications software). This may require rebooting the system, as in the case of CD-ROM Extensions, to load the driver software into memory. One can then begin accessing the CD-ROM drive.

Maintenance

While a purchasing decision should consider the equipment's dependability, even the most reliable hardware will fail or malfunction on occasion and need service. Vendors may repair or replace any equipment they "bundle" with subscriptions to their services.

The buyer, however, should determine this before ordering.

Otherwise, consumers have the responsibility to maintain any equipment they purchase. While academic libraries may have access to on-campus repair facilities, most will probably want to investigate a service contract with a local dealer to resolve extraordinary or unusual mechanical problems.

Normal daily operations will require some periodic preventive maintenance such as cleaning the discs, dusting the hardware, etc. It will also require somebody to familiarize themselves with the computer, printer, and the optical system(s). This person must know how to reboot the system when it crashes (as it will do on occasion), how to change ribbons or ink cartridges, how to load paper into the printer or clear it of any paper jams, and whom to contact in the event of more serious problems.

It may be wise to appoint a single person to oversee routine maintenance matters to ensure that it does not get neglected. Some librarians may want to use student assistants or volunteers to monitor the system, check out discs, and maintain workstations.

In addition to the hardware considerations just discussed, an administrator needs to evaluate the physical requirements of the system in terms of space, furniture, and any possible site-preparation—especially any electrical connections the systems will need. Some of these improvements may represent capital expenditures such as remodeling, changes to the physical layout, and electrical outlets.

CHECKLIST*

Software

1. Is the disc based on the High Sierra/NISO standards?

2. Does the disc vendor deliver its own device driver? Or does it specify the Microsoft CD-ROM Extensions or some other third-party operating system interface?

3. What maximum error rate does the provider promise?

4. Is the user interface intended for novices, expert users, or both?

5. What functions and features does it have?

6. Does it offer command menus, direct commands, or both?

7. Does it make effective use of color and graphic icons?

8. Is it easy to learn, easy to use, and powerful?

9. Is it appropriate for the intended users?

10. Is the search software intended for novices, experts, or both?

11. How are the files indexed? Are there lists of procedures, authority lists, and journal lists?

12. What is the average access time (sort speed and retrieval speed)?

13. Does it accommodate Boolean searches? Free-text searching? Does it use a thesaurus?

14. Does it have help aids such as clear menu screens?

15. Does it permit saving searches?

16. Is it easy to refine and sharpen queries?

17. Does it display search result statistics? Are they easy to understand?

18. What tests would probe the search software's command of scope and precision trade-offs?

19. How well does the product support post-retrieval processing?

20. Does it provide adequate software tools for post-processing?

21. Can search result files be converted into formats which third-party application programs can process?

22. What types of documentation are included (e.g., operator and user manuals)? Does it include system programmer documentation?

23. How good is the printed and ondisc documentation? How good are the tutorials?

24. Does the documentation consider the needs of both novice and expert users?

25. Is there telephone or dial-up online support?

26. Does the vendor provide optional extra support for an additional fee? If so, does the service offered seem to justify the extra cost?

27. How much does the CD-ROM cost and exactly what does the price cover? Does it cover purchase of the disc or only a license to access it? Does it include unlimited use of everything on the disc or are there restrictions? Does it cover only a workstation license or does it extend to a site license?

28. Is the fee fixed or variable? If the fee is based on usage, what is the buyer's responsibility for measuring use and for collecting and remitting fees?

29. Is there a discount for extra copies or subscriptions?

30. What is the system delivery schedule for receiving updates, etc.? What guarantees does the company offer in case of delays?

31. If there are update options, what is the price difference between monthly and quarterly updates?

32. Must you return the old discs upon receiving an update?

33. Is the information content of the disc already available in some other medium? Is it already owned or accessible in some other format or on another CD-ROM?

34. How does one version compare with another in completeness, currency, and organization? Does the CD-ROM medium add significant value to the information?

Hardware

1. What brands and models of equipment does the product run on? What other computer systems is it compatible with?

2. What operating systems and RAM memory are required?

3. Is the hardware compatible with other available CD-ROM products?

4. How many users and sites can the system support? Can this be easily expanded? At what additional cost?

5. Does the disc vendor mention or specify a particular make of drive?

6. Does the disc vendor specify a particular hardware interface (drive/computer)?

7. What maximum error rate does the drive manufacturer promise?

8. Is the drive internal or external (stand-alone)? If internal, is it full-height or half-height? If it is half-height, does it mount vertically or horizontally? (Vertically mounted drives require mounting the disc inside a cartridge or "caddy.")

9. Does the CD-ROM drive incorporate its own hardware interface with the microcomputer or must the interface be purchased and installed?

10. What is the average "down time" for the system?

11. What maintenance is included in the service contract and how fast can repairs be made?

12. What diagnostic software tools does the drive manufacturer provide to identify problems when the drive does not operate properly?

Miscellaneous

1. Who will use the product? How often? For what purpose?

2. Does the producer have a list of current users that you may contact for opinions and comments?

3. How strong is the vendor organization? Will it be around to update its products and provide customer support?

4. Who would recommend purchasing this product? Who would recommend against it? What are their respective arguments?

---

*Adapted from Miller, David C. (1987). Evaluating CD-ROMs: To Buy or What to Buy? *Database*, 10:3, 41–42. Nancy K. Herther. (1987). A Planning Model for Optical Product Evaluation. *Online*, 10:5, 130.

CHAPTER 3
MANAGEMENT ISSUES

Many of the management issues regarding software and hardware have already been discussed in Chapters 1 and 2. In this chapter we will deal with those issues that involve the systems as a whole such as how they fit in with a library's overall plans, how they impact on other services, balancing equipment security with public access, and user considerations.

Integration with Automation Plans

Potential buyers should consider how the implementation of optical systems integrates with their other automation plans or applications. How will a particular CD-ROM work with existing or planned hardware configurations? Can others access it through an existing local area network (LAN)? Does it require special hardware or software to use it? If so, does the vendor supply it?

Will a particular system be truly cost-effective? Cost-effectiveness relates to cost/benefit and user satisfaction. We can think of it as how much useful information a client receives in relation to the dollar allocation compared to savings in staff and searching time. Added convenience is another factor of cost-effectiveness. A proper study should evaluate these items and consider all alternatives. How many of us know the cost/benefit of any of our library's current operations?

Librarians will need to determine whether or not they will limit involvement in optical systems to only one or two products with a separate workstation dedicated to each application or to build a large collection of discs/systems which may present some problems with compatibility. This latter option will require a considerably higher expense for hardware and subscriptions.

Many libraries may not have the financial means to implement this option and will, instead, find themselves in the situation of running more than one application at a workstation. Some users may find this as simple as exiting from one program back to DOS, changing the disc, and loading the appropriate search software into the computer's memory—much as one switches from a spreadsheet to a word processor. The use of a hard disk drive and batch files can simplify this process.

On the other hand, running several applications at a single workstation could require separate system configurations with different device drivers (located in a CONFIG.SYS file). This necessitates rebooting the computer to load the new configuration into memory. One can minimize this by buying from a manufacturer whose products use a common language and device driver.

Librarians may find that some patrons want to use the microcomputer for other applications as well as for searching CD-ROM products. This may especially hold true for those workstations that support a variety of applications. They will need to develop policies to take this into consideration.

Applications May Determine Location

The application will also determine the workstation's location. Public service applications will usually go in a public service area. But what about multi-purpose products? For example, a library which can afford only one copy of a subscription such as Books in Print Plus or Ulrich's Plus or the EBSCO Serials Directory will need to decide whether to put it in a public service area or in technical services. Regardless of the location, one will need to consider whether patrons or staff have the most convenient access to the CD-ROM.

If the system includes utilities to execute the search against an online database after searching the CD-ROM, it will need access to a telephone line as well as a modem. This may encourage some people to locate it in the same room as the online search services where it can also use the same printer, thus saving some money. Similarly, workstations placed in public service areas may also share the same printer through the use of a switchbox to channel output from one computer or another to the single printer.

The mere availability of space may also determine the workstation's location. Each station requires at least 30 to 40 square feet. Other important considerations deal with: maintenance problems (discussed in Chapter 2); security and access issues; patron assistance, including publicity for the systems and any training or instruction requirements prior to use; and system evaluation. The literature of CD-ROM user studies adequately covers most of these issues.

Impact on Other Services

Decision makers should consider optical information systems as simply one part of a range of information services they provide and integrate them with the use of print, microform, and online sources. We have seen that CD-ROM products generally present *more* current information than print sources do but *less* than online sources. This will have an effect on the library's collection development policies and decisions.

Librarians will need to consider whether they will provide laserbase systems as an *additional* service rather than as a *substitution for existing* services. Will an institution acquire all the laserbases in a given area to perform related tasks? Will it subscribe to only those for patron use or only for staff use?

Librarians must also assess the impact of a CD-ROM system purchase or lease on the existing collections. If one decides to cancel print subscriptions to indexes or information sources, he or she will need to consider the potential impact of the consequences of such an action. On one hand, it may result in unnecessary duplication and expense in having both an optical and paper source. Yet, the added convenience may justify the added expense.

We must also remember that products which have license agreements may stipulate that all CD-ROM discs must be returned if a subscription is cancelled. In such cases the library will find itself without backfiles. Librarians will need to determine whether or not they will maintain backfiles of valuable data and how they will maintain them.

Reading the Fine Print

This raises a crucial issue of disc ownership which the subscriber should determine before purchase and certainly before breaking the shrink-wrapping. This makes it particularly important to read any printed matter clearly visible on the outside of the package—including the fine print—to determine such implicit agreements which become effective upon opening the package.

Librarians will have different options depending on whether the producer retains ownership of the discs and licenses the library to access the information or whether the library actually "owns" the discs. Collection development policies may need to be rewritten to reflect these concerns and related decisions.

The current costs of online searching often remain high enough to deter many librarians from using these mainframe databases in many reference situations. As it eliminates telecommunications costs, CD-ROM allows librarians to provide less expensive service to their patrons. The lower costs may enable them to extend "online" searching to situations and users presently unserved and to teleconnect to online databases only for the most current information.

Effects of CD-ROM on Online

CD-ROM purchasers, however, should not automatically expect online costs to decrease significantly. While CD-ROM technology lends itself to full or partial distribution of bibliographic and index databases out into the field, thus making information previously available only online more accessible to the general user, it may raise awareness of online databases and create a demand for those previously unused services.

Some "regular" online users may find a definite shift in usage from online to disc with a corresponding decrease in total number of online searches. CD-ROM, however, will probably broaden the information horizons of many users who may begin requiring online access to more current information.

Similar assumptions were made when librarians began budgeting for automated systems. They argued that the increased efficiencies would save funds by reducing personnel costs. They soon realized otherwise. Rather than significantly decreasing those costs, automated systems simply contained their unrestrained increase while adding to equipment and maintenance expenses.

Some searches may also require refinement beyond the capabilities of CD-ROM such as very complicated or comprehensive searches. The consequence will be that although the total number of online searches may decrease, their average cost may increase due to their greater complexity and duration. In these cases, any potential savings resulting from shifting usage will be lost.

CD-ROM should require a revision of reference policies and procedures in addition to the collection development policies discussed earlier. It will affect work assignments as questions such as who boots up the system, cleans and maintains the equipment, and fixes paper jams get resolved.

One may also need to consider how the staff will react to learning new systems. Will everyone learn them or will certain people become experts on a few systems?

With increased use of laserbases, we can expect increased paper expenses as users print out large quantities of information and references. This will probably increase maintenance costs and require more staff time to supervise and resolve problems. It will also require some consideration of how to ensure relevant and intelligible search outcomes for the patron.

It may be necessary to incorporate some exposure to CD-ROM in bibliographic instruction sessions or to provide otherwise for user training. These issues are discussed further in the section entitled "Users."

Impact on Other Services

Implementation will also impact on other library services.[1] Interlibrary loan (ILL) requests will likely increase if the system does not match citations against library holdings before displaying the results.

Frustration may result from references to items not found in the library and delays in getting them. On the other hand, the ILL librarian will appreciate the time savings the printouts afford. Instead of coping with incomplete or incorrect citations copied from indexes, librarians now have printouts which contain complete bibliographic citations.

Security and Access

Librarians, among others, have concerns about adequate but affordable security for their systems. They need to address a variety of questions in the adoption and implementation process. Some of these have already been explored in this text, such as the need to determine whether all users will have equal access to the systems or whether only institution-affiliated personnel will use them. Security issues may affect the placement of the equipment and the supervision requirements.

Because of the easy portability of expensive hardware, information providers will need to protect their discs and hardware against theft. They will want to prevent individuals from tampering with the drives and potentially removing the discs.

Some may buy lockable covers or cabinets for the equipment to encase the workstation in a sheet metal casing which contains the keyboard on a hinged compartment that can swing up into the main unit and lock. Others may bolt or secure the equipment to the furniture by means of a cable.

Some may place the equipment in a supervised area or one that the reference desk or circulation counter personnel can easily observe. Others may decide to place the equipment in a separate room which they can lock at night. Libraries with a some degree of supervision report less theft and vandalism than those with totally unsupervised access.

Some librarians have even reported the disappearance of the CD-ROM discs. As a result, they restrict access to the discs by making them available from a controlled service area such as the reserve desk. Others also use locking devices for the CD-ROM drives (such as the locks available for the Philips drives) or control access by means of passwords.

Users

Before purchasing a particular product, librarians should estimate how many prospective patrons will access the information. The level of interest and need will depend on the disc's content. If patrons don't need and can't use the information offered, it doesn't matter how accessible or processible the files may be.

This may also have a substantial effect upon how frequently a disc is used. We know that the average per-search cost decreases with increased use. No CD-ROM product currently on the market has a variable-price structure which charges on the basis of usage. Use estimates would be crucial for budgeting purposes in such a case.

Some institutions may require ongoing justification for retaining expensive CD-ROM services. This will necessitate keeping track of number of searches and user evaluations. Determining the number of users may prove difficult to obtain if the workstation is not in a controlled area. One may compensate for this by keeping the discs at a central check-out point such as a reserve desk or by interposing software to capture data on actual usage. Not all systems accommodate such software, however, and none have yet incorporated it in the software.[2]

Library systems, products, and applications must satisfy the needs of a variety of users ranging from novices to experts. Most computer literature refers to the novice user as a beginning computer user; however, from the librarian's perspective, the novice could come in the form of an inexperienced computer user or someone unfamiliar with the literature of a particular area of study. Similarly, the expert user could refer either to a computer power user or to a subject expert. Most library patrons combine varying degrees of computer knowledge and subject expertise that both the librarian and the CD-ROM system need to take into consideration.

Unsophisticated Users

One must also consider that some users never make the transition from elementary user to power user status. They prefer to keep the security of help screens rather than toggle them off even though they can take up one-third to one-half of the available screen space.

Instead of using PgUp and PgDn keys, they continue to move the cursor one line at a time to scroll through several pages of information. If they cling to such elementary procedures, we should not be surprised that they fail to use function keys, macros, "hot keys," and other advanced features.

I once observed a student taking considerable time executing a search and working with the results in a very inefficient manner. When I offered to show him some short cuts to expedite his work, he rebuffed the offer telling me he had several months' experience working with the database on his summer job.

Evidently, nobody provided much training, if any; neither did he read the manuals or tutorials nor did he show any desire to become more proficient. This kind of attitude may typify many CD-ROM users, especially casual library patrons and computer phobes.

We have some true end-user systems on the market that are easy to use, menu-driven, and do not involve Boolean searching. A much larger group of products have more sophisticated features that make them harder to use. These include Boolean searching, command-driven operation, often accompanied by an "easy mode" that uses menus. These systems target a broader user base.

Finally, there are some "high-end" products which have very complex features comparable to certain online services. These products propose to serve sophisticated users and subject specialists. Their use in a library setting may require a librarian or intermediary to execute or assist in the search or they may require specialized training prior to use.

Patron Assistance

The whole area of patron assistance could represent a very thorny issue for librarians. While many users may agree that most CD-ROM systems require no formal training to operate, some ask for better help screens and many want both online and printed documentation.

Databases vary in their ease of use. In addition to posting basic information (quick reference cards) at each workstation, some librarians may want to make available complete vendor and system documentation along with thesauri for heavily-used services. They may also put up wall posters of system protocols and checklists for searchers.

Some of the more complicated products may require the ability to formulate simple to complex Boolean search strategies, depending on the patron's needs. Such systems may require some type of end-user training such as workshop sessions or computer-assisted-instruction before allowing patrons to search.

Some librarians may make written instructions available at the point of service. Some may use a workbook approach or disk tutorials or even interactive videodisc or CD-ROM tutorials. Others may prefer to hire additional staff or student workers to provide peer instruction or to serve as search intermediaries.

Some librarians may consider requiring patrons to submit their search strategy for review before proceeding with the search. If certain laserbases require intermediary searching, will all reference staff learn all the systems or will certain people become experts on selected ones?

It appears that very few libraries provide any formal training or only give minimal training in the use of CD-ROM systems, leaving it up to the patrons to learn by themselves or along with friends. There has been very little literature about such training included as part of general or subject specialty bibliographic instruction programs.

On the other hand, most users prefer to be left alone to do their searches and seek assistance only when necessary. Trying to limit system use to properly trained users may prove an administrative nightmare for systems located in public service areas.

Unlike online systems which have password control and require special training to learn the command language and search protocols, CD-ROM systems aim to extend online services to the end-user, letting the user do their own searching by eliminating most of the barriers that online creates.

What CD-ROM is Not

In addition to teaching the patrons what the CD-ROM contains and how to use it, librarians should also educate them about what it is not. Many will think that the content of the database is totally available in the library, that it lists every article on their topic, or that it contains the library's online catalog. Signs posted in appropriate places indicating the nature or the product along with its scope and contents may eliminate some of the confusion.

Evaluating User Response

User response to CD-ROM systems is generally positive because they save time and remove a lot of tedium from library research. Although some people complain about slow response time, most would acknowledge that the convenience of use and the reduction of hours or days of research to minutes more than compensates for any delays. The constant use of such systems attests to this.

Some installations report waiting lines. Others report cursing when the system goes down or that users prefer to postpone a search rather than use traditional sources. It's almost as though they forget the existence of alternative information sources. As the novelty of CD-ROM systems wears off and as users become more familiar with them and become more sophisticated researchers, we can expect the early enthusiasm to diminish.

User evaluation might incorporate the use of informal interviews, evaluation sheets handed to a sampling of users, or the interposition of a computer program to gather data after completion of a CD-ROM search. We must also keep in mind that users evaluate products based on their familiarity with alternatives. Using such reports as market research may provide unsatisfactory results in the development of new products. We cannot expect users to request technological features they do not know are feasible.

By the same token, producers often find it difficult to wean users away from features and procedures with which they have become familiar. They seem to refuse to consider new or more efficient searching methods or procedures.

Just as people find barriers to the use of traditional methods of research, they will encounter barriers to the use of CD-ROM systems. Many will not avail themselves of the advanced features of many products on the market. Yet they will experience a certain degree of success.

This indicates that users can still use the system successfully even if they do not do so properly. They will probably find some relevant information in a database even though they may search an inappropriate database or the wrong date range. Several of the issues discussed in Chapter 1 regarding scope and contents of CD-ROM databases also apply here.

Spontaneous and Recreational Searching

Some of the early user studies suggest that the availability of free "online" information is changing the way people use information as evidenced by spontaneous or recreational searching. Some patrons may execute quick searches while in the library for some other purpose or just try out a system to familiarize themselves with it. The lack of a ticking meter seems to encourage browsing and use in marginal situations which would have previously been passed over.

Until multi-user systems appear on the market (some are currently in development), single-user systems will suffer the disadvantages of accessibility by only one person at a time and extended use by some patrons. Queues may develop which may cause frustrations or require the purchase of additional equipment or subscriptions which a multi-user system would obviate. Yet, if one selects a multi-user system, he or she should expect response time to decrease. One would need to evaluate response time to determine if it remains acceptable.

Some systems daisy-chain drives to facilitate multi-file searching across several discs. Other configurations place a different database in each drive to permit access to several products from a single workstation. We have yet to see jukebox devices find their way to the CD-ROM environment as they have in other optical environments such as compact disc—audio (CD-A) and WORM.

On the other hand, one may decide to limit use by establishing time limits, stipulating a maximum number of prints, or requiring appointments. All options will require the development of policies and procedures for implementation. The optimum amount of time may vary according to the product (e.g., number of discs it comprises) and its ease of use and demand.

Some librarians may require patrons to sign up in advance to reserve a block of time to use the system. Others might favor appointing somebody to monitor the system, enforce the rules, and resolve problems. One may also set the terminals at a height which requires users to stand. While possibly decreasing the amount of prolonged use by any one person, it will probably also decrease efficiency and productivity as well as increase frustration and dissatisfaction.

Periodic Evaluation

After addressing the relevant issues related to the database contents, retrieval and indexing software, data access times, costs, standards, security and access, and impact on services, and deciding to buy an optical information product, the decision maker should periodically evaluate its use and cost/benefit to ensure that it remains a cost effective solution to the institution's information needs.

This process involves reviewing most of the same criteria involved in the selection process as well as comparing it with other products. The initial purchase presupposes comparison with print, microform, and online alternatives and a justification for CD-ROM. Periodic evaluation will compare a product with others which have appeared since the original purchase. This may involve products performing a similar function or it may involve multiple versions of the same database.

Comparison will consist in looking at the similarities and differences between the various versions and assessing the significance of those differences. These will cover the same points discussed in Chapter 1—content, organization, accuracy, update cycles, and post-processing support among others enumerated at the beginning of this chapter.

Notes

1. Miller, David. (1987). Special Report: Publishers, Libraries & CD-ROM: Implications of Digital Optical Printing. Portland, OR: DCM Associates; Chicago: American Library Association.

2. Crane, Nancy and Tamara Durfee. (1987). Entering Uncharted Territory: Putting CD-ROM in Place. *Wilson Library Bulletin* 62:4, 28–30.

CHAPTER 4
CONCERNS

Users must realize that not all information lends itself to distribution on optical disks. CD-ROMs do not provide a particularly good medium for reading material; but they do offer an excellent means for referring to massive, frequently consulted, and relatively stable databases.

The data should not be so time-sensitive that it requires frequent updating. It should also have a sufficient number of potential users to make publishing it on optical disk economical, or it should contain such valuable information that individual subscribers would not object to paying their proportionate cost of a limited edition.

Limitations

The main limitation of current methods of optical publishing comes as a corollary to a major strength: the discs cannot be erased. Updating the knowledge base necessitates remastering the discs This is exactly what makes CD-ROM a good choice to use in situations which require data permanency and for databases which need little or no updating. It provides an ideal medium for publishers and libraries who deal in information that they do not want altered or mutilated. After all, books and journals (in print or microform) are essentially read-only media.

Researchers have concentrated on developing erasable discs (read/write) for applications where data change rapidly. However, these individuals find it more problematic to develop a reliable read/write disc than to develop the optical disk. This is due to the inability of accurately accessing and modifying the small portion of the disc surface containing the data.

Manufacturers expect to begin full scale production of erasable magneto-optic drives and media by mid-1988. However, such systems will have definite limitations for the foreseeable future. In addition to their relatively high price (Sony estimates a price of 1 million yen [about $8,039] for the drives and 30,000 yen [about $240] for the medium), the systems will suffer from slow seek rates and slow write rates due to the necessary erase-before-write cycle. This situation will probably not stabilize before 1989 at the earliest.[1]

The Copyright Issue

The primary issue that producers must face deals with copyright matters.[2,3] This involves addressing questions such as who owns the data, how does it get used, and who gets compensated and how? Users should not have to worry about copyright issues with optical disks as much as they do with traditionally-published materials. Producers should have resolved these matters prior to publication and included any royalty agreements in the subscription/purchase price.

A potential buyer's main concern often turns to matters of standardization.[4,5] The lack of standards prevented the early development of a "critical mass" of installed products because people remained unsure of which products to buy, which ones would run on which hardware configurations, etc. Many people who were "burned" by computer purchases that prevented them from interchanging software with other machines or from migrating to better software packages without the often substantial outlay of additional capital for new hardware may have figured prominently in this group.

The development of this critical mass presented the optical information industry with a chicken-and-egg syndrome.[3] Buyers were reluctant to purchase until a substantial number of products proved themselves on the market. At the same time, producers hesitated to develop products until the market base was broad enough to support their development.

Even though we now have standards for the physical format (disc size, diameter, thickness, center hole dimensions, recording density, layout of tracks, and rotational speed) and logical format (organization of information in volumes, files, records, and other data elements for use by the computer),[6] we do not have any standards for applications software. It is unlikely that these will develop.

There still are no standards for graphics on CD-ROM, retrieval software, or for user interfaces. There still is some incompatibility which requires separate software configurations to run on different players. This isn't so bad if one configures the hardware to search only one product. The problem becomes more acute in trying to search a variety of products from several producers.

Even though two discs from two different producers may run on the same drive, they often require separate software with separate

CONFIG.SYS files. This may require rebooting the system to make use of a different disc—a definite nuisance and a deterrent to potential purchasers.

Those early adopters who immediately recognized the medium's potential have a certain vested interest in the technology. They purchased products early when prices usually are at their peak. These individuals want to see their purchases pay off. They have an interest in pursuing the technology and its applications, to make it work in their environments, and to see that others also use it.

These users, however, need to beware that they do not get caught up in the technology and make decisions based on the information delivery medium rather than on its content. Other potential users find themselves tied to systems they have already installed. As a result, their flexibility to adopt this new medium is limited.

Rapidly Changing Industry

Another factor for consideration is the rapid change in the industry that causes confusion in the marketplace. Philips and Sony announce a new format (CD-I) even before a previous one (CD-ROM) establishes itself. The same holds true for CD-I and DVI. This multiplicity of formats confuses the buyer. In this situation, coupled with the rapid changes in an industry which continuously produces new equipment with ever more attractive features, the consumer remains very ambivalent about buying anything. A capital expenditure may become obsolete within a year or two of installation.

A parallel to this leads one to wonder about the future availability of equipment to read the data currently being recorded. As it evolves and adds new features, will the hardware continue to support backward compatibility with systems currently in use? This concern will deter some organizations from adopting optical systems due to the fact that the computer/CD-ROM systems become a necessary intermediary between the user and the data which no longer appear in humanly readable form.[7,8]

The National Archives and Records Administration represents one organization that is wrestling with this issue among others which include the problems associated with paper storage, filing, and maintenance; the need for quick record retrieval for the public; the desire to transport images rapidly with no deterioration in quality; and the need to preserve the many original records now in damaged and poor condition.[9]

The National Academy of Sciences recommends, in a commissioned report, the use of paper or microfilm for archival purposes over optical and magnetic media.[7,10,11] It cites permanence (of the discs and the technologies), standardization, and cost effectiveness as its principal reasons for this.

Data Permanence

The Academy claims that magnetic and optical storage media lack the permanence that high quality paper and microfilm offer. Magnetic disks and tape last only ten to twenty years. Optical disks have an unknown lifetime. Some estimates put it at twenty years or less; others put it at fifty years or more. Paper, when properly made and cared for, and microfilm may last hundreds of years.

With the rapid changes in the industry, we may not have hardware and software available to read the disc years from now. Furthermore, the costs of conversion to optical format are astronomically high for an organization such as the National Archives. It has a large number of documents which rarely get consulted. The space savings and rapid accessibility associated with CD-ROM do not make it cost effective for their purposes. In addition, the maintenance costs to keep all the equipment in working order put another burden on the user which paper avoids.

Software Obsolescence

Another serious issue is that of software obsolescence. The study committee identified seven or eight very complete changes in magnetic tape format over the last thirty years. As software continues to undergo constant revision and upgrade, the user needs to convert any machine-readable data periodically.[7]

The expense of conversion will not prove cost-beneficial in an environment that has permanent information, low-level use, and no need to change or update the data. In such an environment, equipment obsolescence would likely become a serious problem.

Despite optical storage's shortcomings in this regard, the National Archives will use it for some of its records. Researchers have such a high demand for some documents that an optical storage and retrieval system appears to be a favorable solution for these items. This could involve a million documents—a very small percentage of those stored. The Archives is presently interested in optical systems more for experimentation. Preservation is only a secondary concern.[10,12]

William Hooton, director of the Optical Digital Image Storage System Project (ODISS), expects to complete the ODISS research project early in 1989. The $1.1 million contract awarded to System Development Corporation, a systems integrator in California, includes almost 1.5 million compiled military service records of members of the Tennessee component of the Confederate States Army and Navy and selections from the Pension and Bounty Land records and other nineteenth- and twentieth-century holdings. The project aims to gather data on preservation, document selection, document preparation, document input and conversion, document indexing, quality control, document storage and retrieval, and document output.[13]

Data Reliability

Another issue related to the question of data permanence involves data reliability. Anybody who has wrestled with the problem of trying to identify a particular version of a document that has undergone many revisions will appreciate the difficulty of locating certain pieces of data that may have been deleted at some stage of editing and that now prove useful for another purpose. Thus, data lost in revision could mean a loss of access to information without realizing it.

The quantity of storage that optical media provide may compound the problem, especially if the data extend over more than one disc. It is physically impossible for any user to determine the completeness and accuracy of everything contained on an optical disk. As with printed media, the data on the optical medium may be dated or inaccurate by the time of production even though the user or the producer does not realize it.

Multi-Media Discs

Discs that contain multi-media data (text, audio, graphics) present special problems. Since CD-ROM is essentially one long linear medium, it stores data only sequentially even though it permits random access. It thereby presents a problem in the retrieval of several types of data simultaneously. One solution, called "interleaving," uses a checkerboard-type technique for simultaneous access to such information. One sector stores audio, another, graphics. The third sector stores more audio and the fourth refresher graphics, etc.

Data error detection and correction presents another consideration to identify and correct any imperfections in the recording and playback of data as well as to correct errors caused by disc eccentricity and rotational fluctuations. For example, a one-color drop-out in a video frame equals a whole line of lost data in a data record.[14]

Pricing

As the pricing of optical information products remains quite high, some libraries face severe budgetary questions in planning for purchasing or implementation.[15] Very few libraries, if any, charge users for access to printed materials. On the other hand, most pass on to the user the costs of accessing online databases.

What will they do about optical information? Many librarians may need to address anew the philosophical issues of whether or not they should pass on some or all of their costs by charging patrons for access to certain kinds of information.

Producers, on their part, have serious difficulties in determining price structures for this new medium partly based on copyright issues (which imply royalties) and on ownership of the discs and the information on them. Some producers let the customer keep the discs; others require that the client return an outdated disc upon receiving the current version or keep only the last disc in the event of a subscription cancellation. Some have addressed questions regarding secondary users and let the consumer pass an outdated disc to a less affluent library or branch.

The Single User Issue

Optical systems have received criticism for being single-user systems with extended use by some library patrons causing frustrating queues. This could result in a consideration to purchase additional equipment or multiple copies of expensive subscriptions.

Books and indexes are also single-user systems in that they allow use by and accessibility to one person at a time. The big difference is that the CD-ROM user ties up the equivalent of several print volumes at a single time. Multi-user systems or the implementation of jukebox mechanisms could obviate this problem. Regulating access time may also help.

Very few products have retrospective coverage that go as far back as some of the printed materials. It does not appear likely that optical media will replace print or microform for this reason. Each medium has its own advantages in terms of cost, reliability, speed of access or data capture, and long-term storage capabilities.[16, 17]

It also does not appear likely that many of these older materials will prove suitable or economically beneficial to reproduce in optical format because of the high costs of conversion and the limited potential use. Nor will optical information systems replace online information because there will always be a need to have current information as well as the opportunity to access a myriad of databases which get consulted so infrequently that one cannot justify their purchase.

Benefits of Competition

As CD-ROM systems become more widely available, we can expect to see dramatic price cuts and stiff competition. We have already seen this occur with the three versions of ERIC and the many versions of MEDLINE currently on the market. While an increasing number of reviews of such products appear in the literature, potential buyers need to be aware of what to look for when they compare one product with another.

Issues of content and scope of the laserbase, the quality and flexibility of the search and retrieval software, the types of interfaces to the search process and to the special features of the target knowledge base will represent important considerations.[4, 18, 19]

An interview with six industry executives identified several other obstacles to the widespread adoption of CD-ROM technology.[20] These include ways to bring costs down; the role of hypertext in CD-ROM information processing; the impact of CD-I on the market; the potential for vertical markets to become horizontal; the ability to overcome barriers to acceptance by schools; and the effect CD-ROM will have on personal computing.

Producers need to convince consumers that CD-ROM-based information presents a better alternative than the same information delivered in another medium[21] before they can expect to sell drives. Increased sales of drives and the development of techniques to produce CD-ROM discs at a lower cost should contribute to pressure to continue cost reductions for both drives and discs. Work on portable CD-ROM units and increased cellular phone use will encourage companies to develop embedded CD-ROM directories along with them.[22]

Notes

1. Berg, Brian A. (1987). Critical Considerations for WORM Software Development. *Optical Information Systems.* 7:5, 329–333.

2. Miller, David. (1987). Special Report: Publishers, Libraries & CD-ROM: Implications of Digiral Optical Printing. Portland, OR: DCM Associates; Chicago: American Library Association.

3. Seymour, Jim. (1986). Awaiting the CD-ROM Boom. *PC.* 5:10, 87–88.

4. Desmarais, Norman. (1987). The Status of CD-ROM Standards. *CD-ROM Librarian.* 2:4, 11–15.

5. NISO Standards Update. (1987). *CD-ROM Librarian.* 2:4, 15–16.

6. Schwerin, Julie B. (1986). *CD-ROM Standards: The Book.* Oxford, England: Learned Information; Pittsfield, VT: InfoTech.

7. Herther, Nancy K. (1987). Between a Rock and a Hard Place: Preservation and Optical Media. *Database.* 10:12, 122–124.

8. CD-ROM: Revolution Maker. (1986). COINT Reports: Vol. 6., No. 5. Morton Grove, IL: Info Digest.

9. Vizachero, Rick. (1986). Optical Storage Gets Agencies' Attention. *Government Computer News.* 12-5.

10. Billings, Sandra. (1986). Optical Storage Not an Option for National Archives, Study Concludes. *Video Computing.* Sept./Oct., 5.

11. *Preservation of Historical Records—The National Archives & Records Administration Study of Preservation Media.* Washington, DC: National Academy of Sciences.

12. Hooton, William L. (1985). The Optical Digital Image Storage System (ODISS) at the National Archives and Records Administration, in *1985 Videodisc, Optical Disk, and CD-ROM Conference & Exposition*, pp. 90–95. Westport, CT: Meckler Publishing.

13. ———. (1986). An Update on the Optical Digital Image Storage System (ODISS) at the National Archives, in Judith Paris Roth (Comp.), *Optical Information Systems '86*, pp. 153–157. Westport, CT: Meckler Publishing Corp.

14. Isbouts, Jean-Pierre. (1987). A User-Friendly Guide for Videodisc Producers. *Videodisc Monitor*. June 16–19.

15. Tenopir, Carol. (1987). Costs and Benefits of CD-ROM. *Library Journal*. 112:14, 156–157.

16. Giles, Peter. (1987). Optical Disk Applications: Now That We Have Them—What Are They Good For? *IMC Journal*. July–Aug., 22–23.

17. Pemberton, Jeff. (1986). Shooting Ourselves in the Foot...And Other Consequences of Laserdisks. *Online*. 9:3, 9–11.

18. Herther, Nancy K. (1986). Access Software for Optical/Laser Information Packages. *Database*. 9:4, 93–97.

19. Stewart, Linda. (1987). Picking CD-ROMs for Public Use. *American Libraries*. 18:9, 738–740.

20. Luhn, Robert, David Bunnell, and Harry Miller. (1987). PC World CD-ROM Forum. *PC World*. 5:4, 220–230.

21. Weissman, Steven B. (1987). Coping with Change. *Computer Systems News*. 309, S40–41.

22. Helgerson, Linda. (1987). Keep in Touch. *Computer Systems News*. 309, S36–39.

CHAPTER 5
LIBRARY APPLICATIONS

Since The Library Corporation's introduction of BiblioFile at the American Library Association's Mid-winter Conference in January 1985, the library world has seen the proliferation of CD-ROM products. Technical services presented a unique opportunity to information producers because a large bibliographic database of MARC records already existed in the public domain. Companies did not have to expend large sums of money for data to put on the discs. They could concentrate their resources on developing marketable products that provided real cost savings and therefore gained quick acceptance.

Cataloging

BiblioFile's Catalog Production System, the first bibliographic CD-ROM database, comprises four discs containing over three million MARC (machine-readable cataloging) records of all Library of Congress English language cataloging since 1964 and popular titles since 1900. It also includes Government Printing Office (GPO) publications, music, films, maps, and Canadian publications.

It allows searching the database by author, title, author/title, ISBN, ISSN, and, LC card number. BiblioFile also has search qualifiers to identify items by publication year, place, type of material, and author's name. The system allows editing MARC records, creating original ones, displaying the catalog card image, saving edited records, transmitting them directly to another computer system, printing cards and labels, or converting to OCLC-type magnetic tape.

The company developed custom-designed enhancements to BiblioFile which let a library maintain an in-house catalog, establish a multi-station local area network, and print presorted catalog cards. BiblioFile includes special features such as a bar code reader to augment MARC records with circulation information, additional CD-ROM drives, and up to eight additional workstations.

General Research Corporation provides over five million MARC records including English and foreign titles for books, serials, visual materials, music, maps, and archival and manuscripts control on its

LaserQuest database. The five discs include all LC MARC distributed records and over two million titles dating prior to 1968. About two million records have been contributed by General Research Corp.'s customers which include public, university, community college, school, and special libraries. LaserQuest also includes MARC records distributed directly by the National Library of Canada. Each bi-monthly cumulation adds about 150,000 records to the database.

One can daisy-chain up to eight CD-ROM drives to avoid disc swapping. Access to the records is primarily by title with an author qualifier. The system includes several shortcuts to expedite searching. The use of function keys, truncation symbols, and several wild card characters make keying faster. The title search key accommodates up to forty-three characters. For long repetitive titles, the user can enter the last word of the title after inserting ellipses. Also, truncation wild cards will truncate titles or words in a title; and there is no limit to the number of matches LaserQuest can display.

From Carrolton Press to UTLAS

Carrollton Press used optical digital data discs (12-inch discs) for a product called MARVLS (MARC and REMARC Videodisc Library System) which allowed searching one million MARC records. It also had DISCON for retrospective conversion and DISCAT (a version of BiblioFile) for cataloging. The company planned to mount the complete Library of Congress shelflist containing 6.5 million unique titles and announced its intention to offer the entire Library of Congress law collection on a CD-ROM called LAWMARC.

As Carrollton Press became linked with UTLAS following the purchase of both organizations by International Thomson, these products were discontinued with the exception of DISCON and LAWMARC. UTLAS markets DISCON as a retrospective conversion package and offers it to libraries on a lease arrangement. It uses six CD-ROMs mounted simultaneously to eliminate disc swapping. The database consists of about six million MARC and ReMARC records indexed by LCCN (Library of Congress card number), ISBN (international standard book number), title, alternate title, and series titles.

UTLAS also plans to revive LAWMARC as a combined cataloging product and public access catalog. In addition to the Library of

Congress Law collection, it will probably include holdings of other major law libraries in a union catalog.

Videodiscs

Another optical digital data disc product is Gaylord Bros., Inc.'s MINI MARC. It supports up to four standard videodisc players, providing access to more than 3.5 billion characters of online storage. It requires the simultaneous use of two laserdiscs in order to have available the complete database with indexes. Gaylord also has the MARC records for the Government Printing Office publications in its GPO LASERFILE database and a database of 500,000 audiovisual and educational materials from the National Information Center for Educational Media (NICEM).

These products, all in optical digital disc format, form the beginning of Library Systems & Services, Inc.'s (LSSI) Bibliographic Processing Network. (LSSI is a wholly owned subsidiary of Gaylord Brothers.) The company expects to market a CD-ROM version of the Bibliographic Processing Network (BPN) that will provide access to the MARC database and will aim at the small library market.

It also has the PC/MARC system which now features the LC classification system in machine-readable form that may be accessed through a "windowing" feature. It includes all MARC formats—including maps, manuscripts, and serials.

Library of Congress MARC Discs

The Library of Congress's Cataloging Distribution Service (CDS) is working with Online Computer Systems, Inc. on the Disc Distribution Pilot Project. This endeavor, which should last about sixteen months, will provide MARC bibliographic and authority records via disc to internal LC users and end-user libraries outside LC. Online designs the software to process the records in CD-ROM format, produces actual discs containing the MARC files, performs quality assurance testing, and develops system and user documentation.

The Library of Congress has identified four different categories of MARC records as options to consider for inclusion. The first one includes discs of the "complete service" of books, visual materials, maps, serials, and music records. The second option contains "books only" records; the third, only name authority records; and the fourth, subject authority records.

The design phase explored a large number of issues which covered: the identification of internal preprocessing requirements to generate the tape to be used in mastering the disc; the identification of all applications and systems software that must be developed, including necessary indexes; budgetary impacts, including project start-up costs; development costs; ongoing production costs; and pricing of the service during the pilot project; recommendations on the role of CDS staff should play during the pilot project. The design phase also developed recommendations on the establishment of a beta test involving a core group of libraries, vendors, and internal LC units who will use the disc technology in their local environments. This group will work with CDS to evaluate the feasibility and effectiveness of the selected disc distribution application.

During the implementation phase, the CDS will test the discs at LC before marketing them to other libraries. It will evaluate the overall utility of the CD-ROM files to LC's operations and it will investigate the possible expansion of its distribution service to include USMARC records in an optical format.

The prototype of the MARC Subject Authority file (CDMARC Subjects), currently in field testing, includes display of the full ALA extended character set; automatic retrieval of cross-references, including preferred and related terms; full string or keyword searching; hierarchical record structuring; choice of multiple record formats; full USMARC communications record output; and several printing options. CDS hopes to have CDMARC Subjects and CDMARC Names (name authorities) in the library marketplace by the end of 1988.

OCLC CAT CD450

OCLC's CAT CD450, currently in beta testing, will create subsets of its Online Union Catalog (OLUC) to enable librarians to do most of their routine cataloging. The full collection, on seven CD-ROM discs, comprises the Recent Books Cataloging Collection, the Older Books and Most-Used Nonbook Cataloging Collection, and the Authorities Collection.

The Recent Books Cataloging Collection and the Older Books and Most-Used Nonbook Cataloging Collection each consist of two quarterly-updated discs that contain about 1.2 million entries. The former covers the most frequently used records in book format published during the past six years. The latter covers nonbooks and books with imprints predating those in the Recent Books Cataloging Collection.

The Authorities Collection will get semi-annual updates. It consists of three discs and contains the complete file of LC Name and Subject Authority records in a single alphabetic list. Subscribers may purchase it separately or bundled with the Recent Books and Older Books collections.

The CAT CD450 system features context-specific Help screens that the user can access at any time. The help system includes tagging and format information, general cataloging assistance, and steps for using CAT CD450 functions. The software uses windows that allow the user to display and edit related records simultaneously and to transfer text between windows.

CAT CD450 retrieves and processes materials in batch mode. It incorporates an online link to the OLUC to retrieve records not found on the discs and transmits original cataloging for items unique to the library.

Local processing capabilities include searching, checking LC name and subject authorities, viewing catalog card images, editing records and label displays, creating new records, and printing catalog card sets and labels. The system also accommodates searching on some fields not fully indexed in the OLUC including subtitle and technical report number.

OCLC is working on similar CD-ROM subsets for law and medicine and is considering the development of other specialized databases.

The British Library

The British Library is working with the Universities of Birmingham and Loughborough, Hatfield Polytechnic, and the University College London to develop a project aimed at improving the speed and efficiency of information exchange in research communities. The British Library has been working on the project for several years and showed a prototype disc in the fall of 1985.

It contained almost 600,000 records which included samples of

UKMARC, the online version of *British Books in Print*, and the Conference Proceedings Index which is the record of conference publications held by the British Library's Lending division. The project will pay special attention to the problems of indexing data.

Public Access Catalogs

Many libraries began or completed retrospective conversion projects in recent years. They have accumulated sizable databases of machine-readable bibliographic records to which they contribute on a daily basis as they add new materials to their collections. They produced these databases with a view to incorporating them into public access catalogs and circulation systems. Some producers of optical disk products saw these databases as prime candidates for mastering CD-ROM-based public access catalogs.

Brodart produced the first public-access catalog in CD-ROM format under the name of LePac. It originally used a specially designed ten-key pad to provide keyword access to authors, titles, or subjects for the inexperienced user. Experts can also use a full keyboard to search the same keys as well as any word in any indexed field such as call number, LCCN, or publication information. LePac accommodates Boolean searching and can be customized to suit local needs such as displaying full MARC tags or diacritics.

The Intelligent Catalog

The Library Corporation introduced The Intelligent Catalog which begins the search process by asking what the patron wants to find. He or she can specify author, title, or subject or use the dictionary search option to have the catalog automatically display a list that includes these three elements.

The patron does not have to enter an entire word. Typing a single letter produces a list of possibilities on the right side of the screen. As the user enters additional letters, the system automatically narrows the list to reflect what has been keyed. One can stop typing at any time, select an item, and enter the catalog which accommodates Boolean searching on any number of words in the database. In addition to performing dictionary, keyword-in-context, or Boolean searches, the catalog responds to natural language requests and displays records in any of four different formats, including the MARC format.

The Intelligent Catalog provides five levels of use. It has automatic tests to determine the operator's level of sophistication from the responses. These levels range from One in which the user simply points to a selection and utilizes dictionary searching. Level Four (for experienced searchers) provides a minimum of explanation and Boolean searching. Level Five gives librarians access to MARC tags and records. Each library selects the initial level for each workstation. Context-sensitive help screens appear on demand or automatically in response to invalid entries.

As patrons progress through a search, they can make notes on new ideas or other references, create and sort bibliographies, and save a log of their search paths. They can print these on the printer that comes with the workstation or save them on disk for future use. The system also has a bulletin board to alert patrons to interesting events in the library or community and provides on-screen maps that show the entire library or a small section of it.

Librarians can update the Intelligent Catalog from MARC tapes or from BiblioFile diskettes as often as they wish. The update files reside on the hard disk, totally transparent to the user. A single query examines both the CD-ROM disc and the hard disk.

The Tacoma Public Library, in Tacoma, Washington, selected the Intelligent Catalog for its seven branches. It is working jointly with The Library Corporation to develop an interface between the CD-ROM system and its local circulation system. When completed, a single keystroke will indicate whether or not the library has the item available for circulation. The two organizations mutually agreed to place the software in the public domain.

Another feature currently under development by the Del Mar Group is the Reader's Advisory Assistance. It will generate an interest profile for the user and then suggest related works which the reader might find interesting.

MARCIVE's PAC

MARCIVE, Inc. became the first company to use write-once, read many (WORM) discs in a library setting. Because librarians were reluctant to add yet another piece of optical equipment to their inventory, Marcive withdrew the WORM and substituted CD-ROM. A first-time user can retrieve titles right away by author, title, or subject without requiring librarian assistance. Notes (help screens) appear throughout the system to assist searchers in locating information. The librarian may compose or edit these screens to use appropriate language and give examples especially meaningful to his or her patrons.

For the more advanced user, MARCIVE/PAC allows for combination searching by author/title, author/subject, and title/subject. It accommodates Boolean searching with AND, OR, and NOT operators. It lets the user search any or all note fields for keywords or to look for numbers if desired (LCCN, ISBN, ISSN, NLM citation numbers, etc.).

It also accommodates call number searches on the library's own call number or other available classification systems. This is a great feature for union catalogs. The normal display pattern appears as a catalog card image; but the user can get a full MARC record display with MARC field tags, indicators, and delimiters rather than the user-friendly display of the public version. One can also create and print bibliographies.

MARCIVE's update capabilities let the librarian decide how frequently to update the catalog. This involves sending new titles to MARCIVE which processes them and returns to the library a magnetic tape for loading onto a backup drive for subsequent transfer to a hard disk. The Winchester disk holds about 15,000 titles reducing the need to remaster the CD-ROM and provides a totally transparent interface to the user.

GRC's LaserGuide

General Research Corporation's (GRC) LaserGuide automatically expands a query to any word if a subject search results in no matches. It incorporates a musical note in the lower right-hand corner that blinks to indicate that LaserGuide "whistles while it works." It accommodates Boolean searches in addition to the usual author, title, and subject keys and lists additional topics to expand or narrow queries and to explore related concepts without extra keying.

LaserGuide incorporates an instant updatability feature to provide access to new titles which it identifies and displays first. It includes the library's floor plans and instructions to show patrons where to locate their books. It also lets the user browse the shelves without leaving the catalog. GRC also provides customized options to modify the catalog to individual needs and preferences.

WLN's LaserCat and LSSI

The Western Library Network (WLN) developed the LaserCat to make its database of over 8.5 million items available to libraries on CD-ROM. The three discs represent the holdings of more than 200 libraries in the WLN service area.

Library Systems and Services, Inc. (LSSI), introduced Spectrum 200, a public access catalog on CD-ROM developed by Gaylord Bros. and Online Computer Systems, Inc. Online Computer Systems provides the retrieval software, database indexing, access software, disc premastering, and mastering services. The retrieval software allows patrons to browse a library's holdings by author, title, subject, call number, and keywords in author, title, and subject fields.

Additional features include choice of output displays, help screens and a "New Books" browse list for patrons wishing to scan only recent acquisitions. The password controlled search mode allows more comprehensive access to the library's collections by providing additional indexes and advanced search features for the experienced user who can also use full Boolean search capabilities, truncation functions, record saving, and editing features.

AutoGraphics's IMPACT

AutoGraphics, Inc. specifically developed IMPACT as an optical disk catalog, not an add-on to an existing circulation system. It features word search and authoritative cross-reference aids. The basic system permits searching by author, title, or subject and supports browsing in those three indexes as well as by call number. Clients can also obtain upgrades to support complex searches and limit them by publication date, format, language, and location.

AutoGraphics also introduced a CD-ROM version of its Government Documents Catalog Subscription (GDCS), formerly available only on microfiche. It contains the entire Government Printing Office Catalog dating back to 1976 and includes both depository and nondepository items. Users can access citations by author, title, subject, SuDocs number, and keyword.

OCLC's CD/2000

At the 1988 ALA Mid-winter Meeting, OCLC introduced the CD/2000 system, a product that provides a CD-ROM version of a library's LS/2000 public access catalog. It can serve as a backup when the LS/2000 catalog becomes unavailable such as when it experiences problems or during scheduled down time for systems backups or preventive maintenance. It can also provide a convenient means for remote access to a library's database when telecommunication costs are prohibitively expensive or unavailable.

The system employs a sophisticated user interface that supports Boolean logic. Several libraries can share the disc real estate to reduce production costs and use passwords to make their individual databases accessible only to their own patrons. The software is compatible with OCLC's other CD-ROM products.

Interlibrary Loan

The Iowa Locater, developed by both the Iowa State Library and Blue Bear Group, Inc. is designed to assist in interlibrary loan work. The CD-ROM disc contains about 470,000 bibliographic records with 1.1 million holdings. The system permits searching by LC card number, author/title, or a 'classed catalog' approach. One performs an author/title search not from the keyboard but from a series of indexes.

It has two screens with entry points for selection of the one that precedes a particular need. After four such selections, the desired title pops up with the holdings from twenty-six libraries displayed. The classed catalog approach permits selection from the index points, to choose Dewey or LC call numbers.

Brodart Automation's LePac: Interlibrary Loan Option, currently in beta testing, will add electronic mail features to the public access catalog. Each member has the complete database on CD-ROM and can search as often as necessary. The operator stores loan requests and responses on a hard disk and sends them to the Interlibrary Loan (ILL) Director (a microcomputer) for transmission at night to each participating library.

The system receives responses and new requests and stores them in the mail queue. If a response does not arrive after a predetermined length of time, the ILL Director sends the request on to the next library in the queue.

The ILL Director collects and maintains records of ILL and calling activity, errors, and exceptional conditions on the hard disk. It can store up to 50,000 requests, acknowledgments, and related messages as well as track continuous statistics on up to 500 ILL Option workstations. A single ILL Director should place thirty to sixty calls an hour.

Acquisitions

R.R. Bowker, International Computaprint, and Online Computer Systems, Inc., all divisions of Reed Publishing U.S.A. have produced *Books in Print* and *Ulrich's International Periodicals Directory* in CD-ROM format under the name of Books in Print Plus and Ulrich's Plus.

The Books in Print Plus system includes *Books in Print, Books in Print Supplement, Forthcoming Books, Subject Guide to Books in Print,* and *Subject Guide to Forthcoming Books* all on one disc. It does not contain *Paperbound Books in Print,* however.

This system provides access to over 695,000 titles from *Books in Print,* including about 70,000 new ones and about 85,000 soon-to-be-released titles along with full publisher/ordering information from *Forthcoming Books.* More than 602,000 of these titles and all of those from *Forthcoming Books* have cross-references under 63,500 LC headings from *Subject Guide to Books in Print.*

The software permits simultaneous searching of all five publications by almost any criteria: author, title, keyword, publisher, subject, edition, audience, language, price, publication date, ISBN, LCCN, illustrations, and grade level.

It accommodates Boolean logic and stores prior results for later recall and combining with new queries. It also has two different operating modes: one for the experienced user and one for the novice with easy-to-use menus and on-screen help available at a single keystroke. Access time averages one-half second with a maximum of 1 second with a Hitachi disc drive and .7 second with a maximum of 1.1 second with a Sony drive.

The citation window indicates the number of bibliographic records that match a particular algorithm. The system provides for a variety of display formats, including *Books in Print,* LC card image, OCLC, custom, and detailed. After retrieving a citation, the operator can edit it and print order forms or save it to a file for electronic order transmission to Ingram, BroDart, Blackwell, or Baker and Taylor.

Bowker has also released a combined version under the title Books in Print with Reviews Plus. It features book reviews from major trade and library publications (*Choice, Booklist, Library Journal, School Library Journal,* and *Publisher's Weekly*) and provides a combined total of more than 20,000 reviews each year.

Ulrich's Plus

Ulrich's Plus uses the same type of software to access more than 68,000 periodical titles from *Ulrich's International Periodicals Directory* (arranged alphabetically by title in 557 subject categories) and about 36,000 titles from *Irregular Serials and Annuals*. It includes Bowker's *International Serials Database Update* with current information on new titles, title changes, and cessations for more than 6,000 entries each year. It also contains the complete names and addresses of periodical publishers and an ISSN index that lists more than 75,200 current and 13,800 former title ISSNs.

Ulrich's Plus retrieval software accommodates close to twenty different search criteria, including: title, subject, media code, ISSN, frequency, circulation, country code, online vendor, year first published, abstracting and indexing services, status code, price, publisher, and Dewey Decimal number. In addition to basic subject queries, Ulrich's Plus has the extended capability of searching or browsing 1,500 cross-references from the Ulrich's Cross-Index to Subjects.

The company has also released Books Out of Print Plus which covers some 300,000 titles that publishers have declared out of print or out of stock since 1979. Users can search by title, author, subject, children's subject, publisher, keyword, ISBN, price, publication year, series title, illustration, and LCCN, as well as algorithms familiar to OCLC users such as 4,4 author–title and 3,2,2,1 title—either alone or in combination.

As with the other Bowker products, the system supports both Boolean logic and truncation as well as novice and expert modes and a browse mode for quick scanning of the title, author, subject, children's subject, publisher, and keyword indexes.

In addition to developing Macintosh compatible versions of

Bowker's complete line of CD-ROM products, Online Computer Systems, Inc. is working with Buchhandler Vereinigung GmbH to produce *Verzeichnis Lieferbarer Bucher* (German Books in Print) in CD-ROM. It will include a complete international extended character set and have the ability to switch the language of the software interface from English to German or French while the database remains in the original German.

The software will function in a manner similar to Bowker's Books in Print Plus. Online, Buchhandler Vereinigung, and Bowker view this joint project as an effort to establish an international "books in print" software standard which any company working with Online may adapt to produce a CD-ROM product.

David Whitaker, publisher of *British Books in Print,* has explored the possibility of producing both the U.S. and the British versions of *Books in Print* on a single disc. The endeavor has not yet resulted in any product.

Any-Book CD-ROM

The Library Corporation's Any-Book is probably Books in Print Plus's major competitor. The company mastered the database on CD-ROM and collaborated with Ingram Book Company which marketed it under the name LaserSearch. It includes The Library Corporation's Any-Book database of publication information (previously available only on microfiche and now exclusively on CD-ROM), Ingram's own database of in-stock titles, and a publisher's directory.

In addition to providing bibliographic information and publication status for virtually any book published in the United States, the disc incorporates an automated acquisitions system. It automatically converts the data into a purchase order format for printing or for sending to the vendor via telecommunication.

It contains approximately 1.5 million bibliographic records for English language titles currently in print, recently out of print, or forthcoming, as identified by the publishers. The disc also contains name and address information on about 20,000 publishers.

Any-Book accommodates title, author, author/title, ISBN, LCCN, title code, and year range search keys. The user can further limit the search by entering the first two characters of the author's last name or a single year or range of years covering the publication span. He or she can then produce purchase orders and maintain all acquisitions records including fund accounting on the system.

Upon receipt, the user can transfer the ISBN to a special file for use with the BiblioFile Catalog Production System. BiblioFile takes the ISBN and matches it to the appropriate MARC record for cataloging.

While Ingram Book Company has since discontinued marketing the library version of LaserSearch, it continues to support the book store version. The Library Corporation is now the sole marketer of AnyBook. Ingram plans to concentrate its efforts on electronic ordering interfaces. Ingram has also worked with the Del Mar Group to refine its CD-ROM system for bookstores to facilitate identification of title and availability information as well as electronic ordering. A unique feature of this system is the ability to identify misspelled words and to suggest possibilities for selection. Although Ingram has no current plans to produce a library version, it may decide to do so at a later time.

Baker & Taylor's Plans

Baker & Taylor and the Del Mar Group developed a prototype of the Librarian's Inquiry Terminal to test librarians' reactions to a CD-ROM conceptualization of a database combining catalog and review capabilities. The system uses touch screens and artificial intelligence techniques to develop a profile of the reader (including age group, gender, and interests) to generate lists of suggested titles. Users can also search for books by title, author, or ISBN.

After locating an item, the Librarian's Inquiry Terminal shows the dust jacket, the table of contents and first page, and provides information on the author as well as a review of the book. Although Baker & Taylor demonstrated the system mainly to elicit librarians' reactions and has no plans at present to market it, it is working on a CD-ROM product that will most likely serve acquisitions functions.

EBSCO's Serials Directory

In addition to Ulrich's Plus, discussed previously, serials librarians will soon have another option to choose from in *The Serials Directory/EBSCO CD-ROM*. The printed version contains references to over 113,000 serial publications and includes annuals and irregular series, as well as a "Ceased Title" index.

The Faxon Company has loaded over 250,000 records for the entire Library of Congress MARC-S Serials file onto a CD-ROM disc. Users can access the information in seconds by LC or ISSN numbers, title keywords, or author. Faxon links the CD-ROM disc to its MicroLinx serials check-in to allow for instant transfer of the MARC-tagged records to a hard disk and then into the MicroLinx database for serials control. The user needs only to edit or insert library-specific information as all standard information about each title is automatically converted.

Reference Works

Grolier became the first publisher to use optical media (both videodisc and CD-ROM formats) to provide access to its *Academic American Encyclopedia,* already available through online services. The CD-ROM version, called the Electronic Encyclopedia, has far more sophisticated searching capabilities than either the print or videodisc versions. However, it contains only text. The compact disc—interactive (CD-I) version will include graphics (3,000 still and animated pictures) and audio data (a three-hour database of speeches, sound effects, and song) as well.

Using the electronic index, which is almost as large as the encyclopedia itself, users can obtain a list of entries containing a key word or group of words in a matter of seconds. Yet, the encyclopedia and index occupy only twenty percent (110 megabytes) of the storage capacity of the disc.

Oxford English Dictionary

Tri-Star Publishing has produced a CD-ROM version of the *Oxford English Dictionary* which Bowker Electronic Publishing also markets. The search menu relates to the eight indexes that correspond to various elements in each entry: the lemma or headword, definition, etymology, labels or specifiers (such as part of speech, mode of speech, subject category, or place name), and quotation references which include date, author, title of a quoted work, and word or words within the quoted text. Since the system supports Boolean logic, the user may search any combination of indexes in the same query.

The software stores up to sixteen queries indefinitely and can send results to a printer or to a standard DOS file for later use. The operator can save searches for later recall either for repeated use or as the basis for a new strategy that combines several different queries. The user can also add his or her own research notes to the results.

To accommodate multiple users, the program can distinguish among as many as eight different profiles with each one capable of storing individual queries, notes, and files independently. The system uses continuous on-screen prompts and pull-down menus to familiarize the operator with the command options. A single keystroke can provide additional help as needed. The company is negotiating with Oxford University Press for other titles to produce on CD-ROM.

McGraw-Hill Book Company's professional and reference division released the Scientific and Technical Reference Set which combines the complete text of both *The McGraw-Hill Concise Encyclopedia of Science and Technology* (7,300 articles) and the *McGraw-Hill Dictionary of Scientific and Technical Terms* (3rd ed.) (98,000 terms and 115,500 definitions). One of the special features provides the capability of using function keys to highlight words in the encyclopedia text which may be 'looked-up' in the dictionary.

The system also includes digitized images compatible with Reference Technology's DOCUSYSTEM software and hardware for display on a high-resolution monitor or printing on a laser printer. Users without the enhanced RTI system can retrieve and display the ASCII text without images. They can search by any word or phrase to get concise, accurate, authoritative coverage of all the physical, earth, and life sciences plus engineering at the touch of a keystroke.

John Wiley & Sons also have several CD-ROM products which include scientific indexes and dictionaries. These are discussed in Chapter 6 under the heading, "Science."

Pergamon's Compact Solution

Pergamon Infoline produced what it calls a Compact Solution—a comprehensive CD-ROM publishing service. The system allows the full word-processing capabilities of a personal computer to modify and rework text retrieved from the disc. A mouse lets the reader place and size the high resolution graphics to suit individual needs. The first product in the series includes the ten-volume *International Encyclopaedia of Education*.

The Knowledge Retrieval System (KRS) uses pull-down menus and icons. The reader can place "bookmarks" in places to review. One can also consult "path to article" which shows the items viewed on the way to the present article. Pergamon intends to provide 'one stop shopping' for publishers, information providers, and companies wanting to exploit CD-ROM for directories, journals, reference books, manuals, and maps.

Pergamon also publishes *Electronic Publishing Abstracts* on behalf of the International Electronic Publishing Research Centre. An online database of some 20,000 articles dating from 1975, it includes abstracts on word processing, speech recognition and synthesis, electronic mail, copyright, cable TV, CD-ROM, and laser printing.

Reference Technology, Inc.'s Reference DataPlate contains the full-text, unabridged version of the *Random House Dictionary* and *Roget's Thesaurus* as well as the *National Telephone Directory* listing some 200,000 frequently called government and corporate phone numbers. Highlighted Data markets the Merriam Webster Ninth New Collegiate Dictionary on CD-ROM and Sansyusa Publishing Company is working on a multilingual dictionary.

Microsoft's Bookshelf

Microsoft Corp. developed Microsoft Bookshelf, a library of ten reference works stored on a single CD-ROM disc. It includes the entire *American Heritage Dictionary, Roget's Thesaurus,* the *1987 World Almanac and Book of Facts, Bartlett's Familiar Quotations,* the *U.S. Zip Code Directory,* the *Chicago Manual of Style,* Houghton Mifflin Spelling Verifier and Corrector, Houghton Mifflin Usage Alert, Lorna Daniells' *Business Information Sources,* and a collection of more than 100 forms and letters for use as templates. It works with any of fourteen word-processing programs, allowing users to retrieve text from the CD-ROM disc and insert it directly into documents. This is the first CD-ROM product available for the horizontal mass market.

Facts on File, Inc. has a prototype of the Visual Dictionary CD-ROM which integrates audio, graphics, and text on a single disc. The Dictionary, jointly developed by Facts on File and Editions Quebec/Amerique, Inc. of Montreal, serves as an aid to teach foreign language.

Based on *The Facts on File Visual Dictionary,* it contains over 3,000 line drawings illustrating over 20,000 words organized by thirty broad subject areas. It shows the user a picture of the desired item together with its name in both French and English. The user can hear the word pronounced in both languages and print the picture using a dot-matrix printer.

The prototype uses only French and English. The actual product which should become available by mid-1988 will include French, English, and Spanish, with additional languages available later. It is designed to run on an Apple IIe with 128K; however, an MS-DOS version will soon follow.

Facts on File recently released a CD-ROM version of the *Facts on File News Digest* . The annual contains the full text of the *Facts on File News Digest* from 1980 through 1987. The menu-driven software features Boolean operators, full-text keyword searching, and date limitations.

CD-ROM Source Disc

Diversified Data Resources, Inc. (DDRI) plans to ship its CD-ROM Source Disc free with newly-purchased CD-ROM drives as soon as it completes negotiations with various manufacturers. The disc will contain a list of CD-ROM reference works and available applications and samples of the programs running under Microsoft Windows. Access Softek's Dragnet, will serve as the search and retrieval software.

Knowledge Access International produced CD-ROM versions of Sociometrics Corporation's *Data Archive on Adolescent Pregnancy and Pregnancy Prevention* (NATASHA: National Archive on Sexuality, Health and Adolescence) and Research Publications' *Directory of Library & Information Professionals*. The Adolescent Pregnancy Data Archive covers more than 40,000 variables and 82 major studies of teen sex behavior. It aims to help social scientists, welfare workers, and health professionals obtain information that will help them solve teenage pregnancy problems.

ALA and Research Publications

The Directory of Library & Information Professionals contains data on approximately 45,000 library and information professionals compiled with the cooperation of the American Library Association, Special Libraries Association, American Society for Information Science, Information Industry Association, Medical Library Association, and twenty other library and information associations in North America.

Each entry includes name, address, current employer, education, work experience, and special areas of expertise. It accommodates Boolean searching on any field or data element as well as the ability to export information to word-processing or database management software or to the printer for index card reproduction.

UMI's CD-ROM Products

University Microfilms International (UMI) has completed mastering its entire database of close to one million doctoral dissertations. The two discs cover the same material available in the printed versions of *Dissertation Abstracts International* and *Comprehensive Dissertation Index* as well as online through DIALOG and BRS.

The Backfile Edition of Dissertation Abstracts Ondisc consists of two discs covering theses completed between 1861 and June 1984. The first disc includes 700,000 citations from 1861 through June 1980. The second covers 140,000 abstracts and citations from July 1980 through June 1984.

The current edition, introduced in April 1987, contains citations and 350-word abstracts for 87,000 dissertations published from July 1984 through December 1986. Each year UMI will add approximately 30,000 new titles from 475 universities worldwide.

The user can search both discs by keyword (appearing in the title or abstract), author, title, publication year, and degree-granting university. UMI has also begun to market ABI/INFORM and Newpaper Abstracts as part of its Ondisc family of products.

ABI/INFORM Ondisc contains the most recent five years of that database. In addition to a full bibliographic citation, each record includes a 150-word article abstract.

Newspaper Abstracts Ondisc provides citations and abstracts from the current year's issues of the *New York Times, Wall Street Journal, Christian Science Monitor, Los Angeles Times, Chicago Tribune, Boston Globe,* and the *Atlanta Constitution* (with selected articles from the Atlanta Journal). Each subscription automatically includes the *New York Times;* users can subscribe to any combination of the other six titles as well.

Each record contains an article citation; an indication of the type of article, its length, byline, and special features, such as photographs, charts, and maps; and a concise abstract, or, in the case of the *Atlanta Constitution,* an annotated headline. Users can conduct cross-title searches in order to gain simultaneous access to information from several newspapers

Both menu-driven databases include a built-in command line, help windows, and a tutorial. They provide capabilities for Boolean and proximity searching, field limiting and truncation, and the ability to return to previous searches for combining or modification.

Bible Library on CD-ROM

Ellis Enterprises, Inc. contracted with AIRS, Inc. to create the Bible Library on CD-ROM. It will contain at least four different translations: the King James Version, the New King James Version, *The American Standard Bible,* and *The Living Bible* together with a complete concordance. The company is negotiating to add *Today's English Bible,* the New International Version, and the Revised Standard Version. The library will also contain 18 related works, including the six-volume Matthew Henry's *Commentary on the Whole Bible, Zodhiates Hebrew–Greek Study Bible,* and Elwell's *Evangelical Dictionary of Theology.* Full-text indexing and cross-references developed by noted scholars will link the works.

Users will be able to search by topic or by specific words or combinations of words. The Bible Library will include a full-screen side-by-side display of search results, the ability to browse an index of every word in the Bible through a pop-up window, and the ability to record complex queries for later reuse or modification.

REX on CD-ROM

The Foundation for Advanced Biblical Studies (FABS) produced a CD-ROM version of the thirty volumes of *Religious and Theological Abstracts* (RTA) under the title REX on CD-ROM (REX = REligion indeX). It provides author, title, journal, year, and keyword access (or any combination of these keys) to every word in the abstracts. FABS plans to supplement the RTA with current and retrospective coverage of additional journals in the area of religion, theology, and philosophy.

It also wants to include an electronic database of book reviews to cover significant publications for the previous year and retrospectively. The first update should include Richardson's *Index to Periodical*

Literature: 1890 to 1899 and Poole's *Index to 19th Century Periodical Literature*.

Its FEB on CD-ROM (FABS Electronic Bible) serves as an extensive concordance to the English text of the Bible in five different translations (New International Version, Revised Standard Version, Good News Bible, King James Version, and American Standard Version). It provides access to any word anywhere in any or all of the five translations. One can access the context of any record (verse) by moving an arrow key up or down to see preceding or subsequent verses.

The FRB on CD-ROM (FABS Reference Bible) includes eight English translations of the biblical text (New International Version, Revised Standard Version, *Good News Bible,* King James Version, New King James Version, American Standard Version, Living Oracles [NT], and English Septuagint [OT]) as well as the Hebrew Old Testament (Stuttgart edition), the Greek New Testament (UBS, 3rd ed.), and the Greek Septuagint (Rhalfs) in the original characters.

It also contains translations of the *Apocrypha,* Josephus's *Antiquities of the Jews* and *Wars of the Jews,* Lightfoot's *Apostolic Fathers,* the *Wycliff Bible Encyclopedia, Naves Topical Bible,* and six volumes of language study helps (*Grammatical Directory of the Greek New Testament, Greek/English Interlinear, Greek-English Dictionary, Grammatical Directory of the Hebrew Old Testament, Hebrew/English Interlinear, Hebrew-English Dictionary, Vine's Expository Dictionary of the New Testament,* and *Theological Wordbook of the Old Testament*).

The grammatical and lexical studies provide complete parsing of every Greek and Hebrew word of the biblical text and let the user search for every occurrence of any grammatical form of any word. The comparative search feature lets the scholar move rapidly from one source to another to compare seven different translations of a term in context. This disc comes with the scholar's edition of ChiWriter, a Greek/Hebrew/English word processor that lets the user manipulate the actual Greek or Hebrew characters.

These tools retrieve data within three seconds and let the user save the results to floppy or hard disk.

Future publications will include biblical commentaries; patristics (translations of the writings of the Ante-Nicene, Nicene, and Post-Nicene Fathers along with a few history texts that will provide a reference framework for the fathers and their writings); classic reformation texts (translations of the writings of Luther, Calvin, Zwingli, Wesley and other classics of the Reformation period); classic theological texts of various denominations; classic sermons; classic Jewish texts (all major Jewish writings from the earliest to the twentieth century, including apocryphal and apocalyptic texts, pseudepigrapha, Talmud, and Mishnah); classic apologetical texts; Bible background texts (ancient texts relating to the study of the Bible); biblical maps and drawings (maps and drawings of biblical sites including major archaeological texts and a textual description of each name and place with a note on its significance); and English Bible translations (containing all the major English translations of the Bible from Wyclif to the Geneva Bible, King James to the Revised Version of 1881).

Tri-Star Publishing plans to release a Biblical Reference Library sometime in mid-1988. It will feature three versions of the Bible plus six to twelve reference books.

Indexes and Abstracts

CD-ROM technology presented an ideal medium for publishing bibliographic and index databases for full or partial distribution. Information Access Company (IAC) became the first company to enter the index market with the videodisc version of *Magazine Index* called InfoTrac. It added Disclosure and Ward's Business Directory databases as well as the full text of the *Wall Street Journal*.

The database also includes the *Government Publications Index,* the first patron-oriented current index on videodisc covering documents published by the U.S.G.P.O. It allows users to search by subject, title, author, or issuing agency. It uses the Library of Congress subject headings as well as a complete system of cross-references. The CD-ROM version goes under the name InfoTrac II.

IAC also introduced the Academic Index which includes references to more than 375 periodicals covering education, history, arts, sociology, psychology, literature, political science, religion, anthropology, geography, and computers as well as Asian, Middle Eastern, Eastern European, African, and Latin American studies.

The CD-ROM database also includes citations to articles from the most recent six months of the *New York Times*. It indexes more than 190 publications for the first time as a response to the requests of academic librarians. The remainder of the database represents selected titles contained in IAC's Magazine Index. The company aims to deliver an affordable reference system to provide college and university libraries with single stop searching for periodical literature on academic subjects.

InfoTrac Reference Center

The company also offers SilverPlatter Information Services' and Disclosure's products on its new InfoTrac Reference Center. The system lets librarians network up to eight terminals to provide access to as many as sixteen CD-ROM drives and eight videodisc players. It also supports dial-out access to remote databases from all or any of the terminals on the system.

The system uses the data provider's standard software for search and retrieval. IAC provides the necessary software and hardware to run the network interface. It is negotiating agreements with several other publishers and distributors of widely-used reference databases.

DIALOG OnDisc

DIALOG Information Services soon introduced its DIALOG OnDisc line of CD-ROM products. Its first offering provides the ERIC database which comes as a current file, with one disc containing data from 1980 to the present or as a complete file with two discs going back to 1966. The system offers two search options: DIALOG command language and Easy Menu. The entire product line uses the same or similar command language as the online system.

The Easy Menu option for novices is basically self-explanatory. During a query, the screen highlights the search terms or displays them in color on a color monitor. The user can sort information before displaying or printing it and can transfer results to another personal computer software program for further manipulation.

The system lets users switch from the disc to online without retyping the search strategy. This provides more recent information and the ability to do additional searching in any of DIALOG's other online databases without interrupting the original search.

Recent enhancements make all their CD-ROM products compatible and provide new menu options and expanded search capabilities such as cascading which retrieves all items falling under a particular alphabetical or alphanumeric prefix.

DIALOG OnDisc MEDLINE

DIALOG has released MEDLINE as its second product in the DIALOG OnDisc line. This disc contains the most recent years of the National Library of Medicine database which covers virtually every subject in the broad field of biomedicine. The online version of MEDLINE provides access to more than five million records from 1966 to the present. DIALOG also plans to add other key databases from a variety of disciplines to its DIALOG OnDisc product line.

The third product, NTIS, consists of the most recent four years (1984 to the present) of data. DIALOG plans to produce another disc during the first quarter of 1988 covering 1980 to 1983. The database consists of U.S. government-sponsored research, development, and engineering reports and analyses prepared by federal agencies, their contractors, and grantees.

Some 240 U.S. government agencies use it to make available unclassified, publicly available documents. Some state and local government agencies also contribute to the database.

After executing a search strategy on the CD-ROM file, the user can switch to online to yield additional, current information from the latest updates or other relevant databases or to locate older material.

SilverPlatter Information, Inc.

SilverPlatter Information, Inc. has come out with a number of new products in the last year. Together with H.W. Wilson, it holds the distinction of having the largest selection of CD-ROM discs on the market. Its offerings include:

1. ERIC (consisting of Resources in Education (RIE) and Current Index to Journals in Education (CIJE) from 1983 to the present with quarterly updates).
2. PsycLit (two discs covering 1974 to the present with quarterly updates), containing journal citations with abstracts in psychology and behavioral sciences from the psycINFO

department of the American Psychological Association.
3. EMBASE (Excerpta Medica, three discs covering 1983 to the present with quarterly updates).
4. AV Online (formerly NICEM: National Information Center for Educational Media). It contains the complete database of audiovisual materials from the National Information Center for Educational Media.
5. Sociofile comprises an index to and abstracts of the world's journals in sociology as compiled by Sociological Abstracts since 1974. It also includes enhanced bibliographic citations for dissertations in sociology and related disciplines beginning with 1986.
6. CaCD (Cancer Abstracts) includes references, abstracts, and commentaries of the world's literature in cancer and related subjects from Elsevier Science Publishers, Year Book Medical Publishers, and the National Cancer Institute in conjunction with the National Library of Medicine. SilverPlatter has merged duplicate citations into one record while preserving information that is unique to each information provider.
7. MEDLINE on a SilverPlatter includes the most recent five years of bibliographic citations and abstracts for the complete MEDLINE database. The discs will get remastered annually to reflect changes in the MeSH descriptors.
8. NTIS on a SilverPlatter which includes the most recent five years of the complete NTIS (National Technical Information Service) database of bibliographic citations to government sponsored research and development reports. It comprises: NTIS: Environmental Health and Safety, NTIS: Computers, Communications, and Electronics, NTIS: Medicine, Health Care and Biology, and NTIS: Aeronautics, Aerospace & Astronomy.
9. LISA (Library & Information Science Abstracts), Europe's first fully commercial abstracting service on CD-ROM, providing abstracts of literature covering librarianship, information science, online information retrieval, new information technologies, and publishing. The disc contains over 81,000 citations from 550 periodicals published in over thirty languages. It accommodates truncation, Boolean, proximity, and full-text searching in all fields. It also includes context-related help information to guide first-time users.
10. OSH-ROM, the company's first product to combine several databases from different vendors on the same disc, includes information from NIOSHTIC, produced by the National Institute for Occupational Safety and Health; HSELINE, produced by Health and Safety Executive, Library and Information Services in the

United Kingdom; and CISDOC, produced by the International Labour Office of the International Occupational Safety and Health Information Centre in Geneva.
11. AGRICOLA, a bibliographic database consisting of records for literature citations of journal articles, monographs, theses, patents, audiovisual materials, and technical reports relating to all aspects of agriculture. The National Agricultural Library in Beltsville, Maryland, supplies the data. The current disc contains information from 1983 to the present. The retrospective disc covers the years 1979 to 1982.
12. Compu-Info provides reference data on 12,000 computer products from 1,500 companies.
13. ChemBank, a combination of three major databases on hazardous chemical information, includes: RTECS, the Registry of Toxic Effects of Chemical Substances, from the National Institute for Occupational Safety and Health. It contains identification, toxicity, and general information for more than 87,000 chemicals and 310,000 compound names.

CHRIS, Chemical Hazard Response Information System, from the U.S. Department of Transportation contains detailed information to assist with emergency response, accident prevention, and safety procedure design in the transportation of hazardous chemicals. This file covers more than 1,000 key chemicals.

OHMTADS, Oil and Hazardous Materials-Technical Assistance Data, from the U.S. Environmental Protection Agency. It contains numerical data and interpretive comments that facilitate rapid effective response to emergency spills.
14. Corporate and Industry Research Reports (CIRR), a cumulative index with abstracts to over 70,000 corporate and industry reports written by securities and investment banking firms from 1979 to the present.
15. Business Software Database lists more than 10,000 software packages for business professional, and technical applications. Each record includes a 250-word description which gives name, address, and phone number of the manufacturer; hardware and operating systems information; programming languages; prices; potential users; date first available; installed base; related packages; and other services available from the producer.

WILSONDISC

H.W. Wilson's WILSONDISC line includes:

1. *Applied Science & Technology Index*
2. *Art Index*
3. *Biography Index*
4. *Business Periodicals Index*
5. *Cumulative Book Index*
6. *Education Index*
7. *General Science Index*
8. *Humanities Index*
9. *Index to Legal Periodicals*
10. *Library Literature*
11. *MLA International Bibliography*
12. *Readers' Guide to Periodical Literature*
13. *Social Sciences Index*

The *MLA International Bibliography* database, the newest member of the WILSONDISC family, contains over 230,000 records dating back to January 1981 and adds some 40,000 entries annually. While the online version gets updated monthly from November to June and September, the CD-ROM version will have quarterly updates. Wilson is also negotiating to produce a second CD-ROM which will hold all the historical data (1921–1980).

During the first half of 1988 Wilson also released five new databases in the Wilsondisc series. The titles include: *Essay and General Literature Index, GPO Monthly Catalog/Index to U.S. Government Periodicals, Biological & Agricultural Index,* and *Book Review Digest.*

The software operates similarly to that of Wilsonline or Wilsearch. It features standard Boolean operators, neighboring, conceptual aids, truncation, ranging, and search qualifiers. It provides the ability to automatically continue the search online through Wilsonline. It has two modes for the end-user (browse and Wilsearch, a menu-driven system) and two modes for advanced searchers (Wilsonline for native-language searching and Expert).

The browse mode provides the same access points and capabilities available with the printed indexes by subject headings along with a full set of "see also" references. The user can expand a term to get related ones and page up or down to move up and down the alphabet to view retrieved items. It also allows printing of individual citations. Screen options can be tailored to limit access if desired.

96 *The Librarian's CD-ROM Handbook*

The Wilsearch mode uses the same menu options and search formulations currently available through Wilsearch online. It allows searchers to execute their strategies on disc and then locate subsequent information online. It permits downloading of citations and disconnects automatically.

Wilsearch provides the ability to modify or retry the most recent search in the same or different database. It accommodates author, title, journal, organization, Dewey number, earliest and latest date searches as well as three subjects at a time. The user can also link queries to others by using the term "any."

The Wilsonline mode offers the same search capabilities and commands used with Wilsonline including Boolean logic, truncation, and printing commands. It also has an online thesaurus. The expert mode offers the same capabilities as Wilsonline but with expanded screen handling and windowing functions and a continuous view of search strategy development through the use of a log screen—all without prompts.

PAIS on CD-ROM

Public Affairs Information Service, Inc. markets PAIS on CD-ROM. It contains over 250,000 records beginning in 1972 and indexes worldwide information on public affairs from a variety of sources, including books, pamphlets, government publications, reports of public and private agencies, periodicals, and conference proceedings.

The product's search software, designed by Online Computer Systems modifies that used in Bowker's Books in Print Plus. Novice searchers can use a menu-driven search system while more sophisticated patrons can utilize a command mode. It includes a thesaurus as well as automatic pop-up windows that contain "see" and "see-also" references. The disc also includes a directory of publishers and periodicals giving names and addresses and additional indexes and access points not found in the online version.

The Institute for Scientific Information (ISI) has a CD-ROM edition of *Science Citation Index* (SCI) which will be discussed in Chapter 6. It is the world's largest interdisciplinary science index.

Search CD450

OCLC, Inc.'s Search CD450 package contains bibliographic and citation databases obtained from several sources supplemented by specially created, subject-related subsets of its Online Union Catalog (OLUC). Its first offering includes three databases on five separate discs: ERIC, including Current Index to Journals in Education (1982–present) and Resources in Education (1982–present); Current Index to Journals in Education (1969–1981); Resources in Education (1977–1981); Resources in Education (1967–1976); and Education Materials in Libraries, education-related bibliographic records from the OLUC representing all types of materials. This latter feature includes cataloging information which has only been segmented by subject to increase the hit rate. (OCLC aims to achieve a hit rate of 80 percent.)

Search CD450 includes Education Materials in Libraries (EMIL) in addition to ERIC. It contains over 450,000 bibliographic records pertaining to education, including over 17,000 entries for items printed prior to 1900 as well as listings for manuscripts, machine-readable data files, software, A-V materials, music scores, maps, games, flash cards, slides, sound recordings, filmstrips, and more. It represents a comprehensive collection of education-related bibliographic records for all types of materials printed during the twentieth century.

The Agriculture disc includes the complete AGRICOLA database back to 1979, CRIS (Current Research Information System), and the Agriculture Materials in Libraries (AgMIL) databases. AGRICOLA contains 2.5 million citations to general agriculture and specialized fields compiled by the National Agricultural Library and cooperative institutions.

CRIS, produced by the Cooperative State Research Service of the U.S. Department of Agriculture, includes over 30,000 abstracts and progress reports covering active and recently completed research on agriculture and related sciences. AgMIL, compiled from the OLUC, represents materials pertaining to agriculture, food production, forestry, fisheries, and veterinary medicine in all formats. It covers primarily the twentieth century but includes references to items printed as early as 1537. The series comprises four CD-ROMs. One disc includes current files for AGRICOLA and CRIS while two others contain the retrospective AGRICOLA files for 1983–1985 and for 1979–1982. The fourth disc contains the AgMIL database.

Science and Technology Series

The Science and Technology Series consists of NTIS and three databases from the OLUC: computers, energy, and environment. NTIS covers two discs: the current (1986–present) and retrospective files (1983–1985). Science and Technology Materials in Libraries provides comprehensive coverage of computers, environment, and energy. The records are compiled by reviewing the complete OLUC and using appropriate criteria, including call numbers and subject headings, to identify the items for the subject database.

The Search CD450 interface displays basic options on the screen at all times as function key values. It has user-friendly menus, prompts, and context-sensitive help keys. The system operator can set it to default to a brief, full, or MARC tagged record while the searcher can define his or her own interface.

The software incorporates Boolean logic, control vocabulary or free-text searches, an index or thesaurus, and a search history which can list the last twenty strategies in the current session, including the number of records retrieved, at any time. The operator can easily select previous results and incorporate them in a new search. The searcher may also print records or save them on floppy or hard disk.

Recent enhancements let the user chain up to four drives to search the discs simultaneously. This capability allows librarians to install either a complete database such as ERIC or a combination such as the current ERIC disc and EMIL. A selection menu lets the operator choose the database to search. With just three keystrokes, the user can save the strategy for use on another database without rekeying or changing the disc.

Version 2 incorporates additional search fields, such as LC and Dewey decimal call numbers, U.S. government Document numbers, technical report numbers, and music publisher numbers. It also includes a double-posting feature that lets users locate both subjects and free-text phrases with a single query. It displays results in reverse accession order. This change replaces the relevancy score and graph feature of Version 1.0.

Search CD450 also provides an online module which stores queries with no hits to execute a batch search on OCLC's database in off-peak hours and later download the data to the local database. It also captures local information for uploading to the Online Union Catalog for resource sharing and provides the ability to print catalog cards.

The Resource Sharing component permits the merging of databases from various sources (as long as they're in some type of machine-readable form) to create a union catalog with bibliographic and location information, for example. It can print ALA ILL forms, to support electronic mail for ILL e.g., ALANET and to link with OCLC's online system for interlibrary loans.

ABI/Inform and Newspaper Abstracts

University Microfilms International introduced ABI/Inform Ondisc and Newspaper Abstracts Ondisc. The former contains the most recent five years of ABI/Inform. Each record includes a 150-word abstract in addition to a full bibliographic citation. The latter covers the current year's issues of the *New York Times, Wall Street Journal, Christian Science Monitor, Los Angeles Times, Chicago Tribune, Boston Globe,* and the *Atlanta Constitution* (with selected articles from the *Atlanta Journal*). Each subscription automatically includes the *New York Times*. Subscribers can also select any combination of the other six titles.

Each record contains a bibliographic citation; an indication of the type of article, its length, and special features, such as photographs; and a concise abstract, or, in the case of the *Atlanta Constitution,* an annotated headline. Users can also perform cross-title searches to gain simultaneous access to information from several newspapers.

Both menu-driven databases have capabilities for Boolean and proximity searching, field limiting, and truncation as well as the ability to return to previous searches to combine or modify them. The user interface features a command line, help windows, and a tutorial.

The NewsBank Electronic Index provides bibliographic access to over 500,000 current issues and events articles. It contains nearly five years of index information for *NewsBank, Names In the News,* and *Review of the Arts* (current newspaper review and articles on theater, film, art, music, literature, and television). One types a term to get into the index. A single keystroke refines the search.

The index displays the number of articles cited under a particular term to determine whether further strategies are desirable. A single keystroke provides access to cross references to locate related information or to be taken directly to a "see" referenced screen. Another keystroke accesses the user-friendly Help screens. After retrieving the citations, the user can print them to retrieve the full text on the microfiche. The printout contains full citation information for the NewsBank microfiche of full-text articles from some 300 U.S. newspapers.

LC Pilot Project

The Library of Congress's Disc Print Pilot Project uses a videodisc in a digital imaging and retrieval system. Planning and design began in the early 1980s and production started using the specially-built prototype system in January, 1985.

The modular design permits adding or changing hardware components as the technology advances. Current hardware includes two page scanners, one microfiche scanner, a jukebox for storage of up to 100 videodiscs, ten image display terminals, one batch printer, and two convenience printers.

Users search, identify, and select documents online using SCORPIO commands to access SCORPIO optical disk files. The terminals also allow for local and offline printing. During the course of the Print Pilot Project, between 500,000 and one million pages of text will be scanned. The digitized images are being stored in black-and-white halftones for reasons of economy. One disc can hold 10,000 to 15,000 pure text images per side, but only 110 full-color images.

Current material being scanned comes from the BIBL (bibliographic citation) file and *Congressional Record* (CR 99). The BIBL file includes material from seventy-five periodicals for which the project secured copyright permissions from publishers. There are now about 4,000 BIBL documents available for retrieval in the optical disk print database. The CR 99 file includes issues of the *Congressional Record* from January 3, 1985 to the present.

The public service staff working with the print project felt that this was an excellent candidate for transfer to optical disk since it is a publication which receives generally heavy use throughout the library and appropriate online indexing already existed which covers all portions of the printed record—House, Senate, Daily Digest, Extension of Remarks, and House Lobby. The index cites legislative activities, major statements, and statements made by members on the floor. Items of interest can be located by using a variety of search techniques: subject or keyword, member, date, bill, committee, public law number, recorded votes, and report.

Access to the BIBL file is at the article level. The Serials File will be accessed at the issue and article level using both in-house and commercial indexing (*Magazine Index*).

CHAPTER 6
SPECIALIZED APPLICATIONS

Although libraries presented optical publishers with a large market opportunity, they did not represent an exclusive one. Many other industries require quick access to large quantities of data for which CD-ROM presents an ideal medium of distribution. While the general reference works, abstracts, and indexes we discussed in Chapter 5 target libraries as their primary market, some can find a secondary clientele in the industries we look at in this chapter. Likewise, while the applications we examine here cater to special needs and specific subject areas, reference and special librarians will undoubtedly have an interest in many of them.

Business

The business community provided a large market for optical information products. This, coupled with a significant number of databases in magnetic format, made business applications a logical early application. Disclosure produced a CD-ROM version of the Disclosure/Spectrum Stock Ownership Database which provides detailed and summary stock ownership information for over 5,000 publicly-held companies through an agreement with CDA Investment Technologies, Inc. of Silver Spring, Maryland.

Each record on the disc lists the name, most recent shares traded, and total number of shares held by institutional holders, five percent beneficial owners, and inside owners. This information is abstracted from the reports which individual and corporate shareholders file with the Securities and Exchange Commission (SEC). They include annual and quarterly filings on Form 13D, 13F, 13G, 14D-1, and Forms 3 and 4.

Datext's Corporate Information Database became available in January, 1986 under the name CD/Corporate. The service combines business information from six leading database publishers: Business Research Corp. (the complete text of investment analysts' reports on companies and industries from the Investext database); Disclosure Information Group (the complete contents of the Disclosure II database, also available from Disclosure under the title Compact Disclosure); Data Courier (the most recent three years of abstracts from the ABI/INFORM database also marketed by University Microfilms International); Media General Financial Services (stock price and volume data from The Market File); Predicasts (the most recent two years of abstracts from the Promt database); and Who's Who in Finance and Industry from Marquis Who's Who.

CD/Corporate is a menu-driven system that includes numeric and textual information on all public companies traded on the New York, American, Over the Counter, and regional exchanges. This includes more than 10,000 companies, 900 lines of business, and more than 50 industries and 8,000 executives.

The service also includes comprehensive business information such as company financial statements, excerpts from annual reports, 10-K's and 10-Q's, investment analysts' reports, biographies of officers and directors, and article abstracts from more than 700 journals and periodicals. The four CD-ROMs which comprise this database organize the information by company and industry.

A user can retrieve the information in standard report formats, print it out directly, or transfer it into the most commonly-used business software such as Lotus 1-2-3, MultiMate, or WordStar. The system allows comparison of corporate financial data over time, between firms, and within a user-defined portfolio of as many as sixty companies. The information on each disc dates back seven years and is updated monthly.

CD/Corporate, release 1.1 includes several features that significantly increase the amount of information available to users while also expanding the depth and scope of reports that can be generated. Major enhancements include an increase from three to seven years of historical financial data, customized reports that allow users to develop rankings of companies by industry, line of business, or a custom-built portfolio, using up to fifty-seven criteria, and expanded portfolio features, including the ability to build and research a portfolio of up to sixty companies and save that portfolio for future use.

Datext's CTIS

Datext's second product contains the Corporate Technology Information Services (CTIS) databases on high technology companies under the name CD/CorpTech. This directory includes information and indexes on

Specialized Applications 105

more than 12,000 public and private high technology companies in the U.S. and on over 40,000 products. It contains facts about business description, company status (public, private, subsidiary, or division), address and phone number, names and titles of senior executives, revenue range, and product information.

CTIS also includes menu-driven software which allows a searcher to retrieve and screen information based on any combination of twenty criteria, such as product type, company name, region, state, zip code, area code, annual revenue, and so forth. The user can also download information to an in-house software package for manipulation.

Datext collaborated with Dow Jones & Co. to produce CD/Newsline, the first business information product to integrate CD-ROM databases with online news and information. Subscribers must already subscribe to the CD/Corporate Database. The basic configuration includes a subscription to one disc, monthly updates, an optical disk drive for an IBM PC or compatible computer, search and retrieval software, complete documentation, and Datext service and support at an annual cost of $14,100. CD/Newsline fees range from $4,500 for fifty connect-hours on the four Dow Jones News/Retrieval databases to $53,000 for 1,000 connect-hours.

Datext began marketing several new products before Lotus Development Corporation acquired it and Computer Access Corporation, the developer of the CD-ROM search software BlueFish, in October, 1987. It still remains unclear whether or not the Datext name will continue to be associated with this line. Products include CD/Private+, CD/International, and CD/Banking. CD/Private+ provides detailed financial information on almost 120,000 private U.S. firms arranged by industry or line of business. It includes those companies covered in *Ward's Business Directory* and Macmillan's *Directory of Leading Private Companies* listing the 6,000 most successful privately owned firms in the U.S.

CD/Private+ also includes current financial data on selected public companies as well as detailed information on the 6,000 most successful private corporations in the U.S. The profiles for each firm give full identification of address, telephone number, year started, type and identification of ownership and CEO, with revenue, number of employees, description of business, and SIC code.

The public firms have additional financial data, such as ratios and balance sheet items. The private companies described by the Macmillan database offer more detailed financials, such as assets, liabilities, and net worth; number and type of facilities; listings of ten to fifteen corporate officers; service firms to the listed company such as law, insurance, accounting firm, and bank; and even the telex number.

The proprietary menu-driven software resembles that of CD/Corporate and features the ability to screen companies using up to ten of 145 selected criteria for private firms and a set of seventy-four criteria for public corporations. It also permits selecting companies based on SIC codes or industry description, locating executives with titles and addresses, and a portfolio capability for side-by-side comparative analysis of up to 100 firms.

CD/International

CD/International comprises an integrated database of some 2,000 U.S. and 2,000 European and Japanese large, publicly traded corporations. It provides more detailed financials than do the other products developed by Datext; but it does not initially include news or extensive textual commentary. Some fifty financial analysts from two data suppliers have joined forces on the database: Wright Investors' Service, a money management and financial data publishing firm and CIFAR (Center for International Financial Analysis and Research), a group known for its analytical expertise with international accounting procedures.

CD/International is unique in that it represents 200 items of financial data in native form according to national accounting procedures. This includes eighty-two fundamental and sixty-five computed financial variables based on company reports, descriptions of thirty-two types of company-specific accounting practices, as well as business descriptions and share price information. It thus enables accurate and direct comparisons between firms with different accounting practices. The 4,000 corporations from twenty-four countries represent eighty-five percent of the total world market value.

The software, while similar to that of the other related products, has added features for this type of data. Automatic translation into any currency at any exchange rate and powerful reporting capabilities complement the proprietary screening program called ScreenSheet which allows users to sift through the data using any combination of the 200 variables to pinpoint corporations matching the required characteristics. The disc organizes the businesses under twenty-five industry categories.

While Datext planned to release a similar database called Worldscope in an online format, it has no plans to combine CD/International with the online product since the CD-ROM will contain just as timely information.

CD/Banking

CD/Banking includes a series of products covering the banking industry. The first disc contains the Commercial Banks Database which comprises data from Sheshunoff & Co. on 14,000 bank call reports with more than 300 variables on federally insured U.S. banks compiled by the FDIC and Federal Reserve Board. These variables include deposits, loans, and profits, noninterest income, liquidity, overhead, nonperforming loans, and growth and market share data with rankings and ratings. Coverage includes annual data for the past six years and the eight most recent quarters.

The software permits screening on the 300 variables for specific analysis, the development of a portfolio showing data on numerous banks side by side, and regional selectivity for competitive and merger analysis. The user can then rank completed analyses according to any of these criteria.

Lotus Development Corp. has a series of financial databases on CD-ROM under the name One Source which provides access from one to eight databases on a single disc. These files include Daily Stock Price History, Compustat, Value Line, I-B-E-S, Bonds, Ford Investor Services, Financial Post, and Disclosure II.

The system which integrates with Lotus 1-2-3 software and Microscan, an integrated investment research and portfolio analysis program, will serve as the foundation for the company's financial workstation which will integrate real-time pricing information and personal computer applications.

Standard and Poor's Compustat financial database on CD-ROM covers more than 10,000 U.S. public companies (7,000 active firms) with 15 years of annual financial data; 10 years of monthly price, dividend, and earnings data; 7 years of business segment and demographic data; SIC codes; officers; 15 years of archival data on inactive companies and those which file independent reports; and 15 to 20 years of industry aggregate data. The company markets the product as a fully-integrated financial analysis package with easy-to-use software that allows screening, report generation, downloading to spreadsheets, and the ability to add and merge one's own company data.

Dun & Bradstreet Prototype

Dun & Bradstreet's Information Systems developed a CD-ROM prototype for internal operations only. If it proves successful and marketable, Dun & Bradstreet may eventually make it available to the public. They intend to distribute to their information customers financial and business data (the D&B business information database) on CD-ROM that is now only available online.

Several D&B companies have been working on developing their own prototype systems and experimenting with several different CD-ROM vendors, including Reference Technology, Inc. and LaserData.

Donnelly Marketing Information Services's Conquest Consumer Information System consists of several software components which provide a variety of data analyses:

- AmericanProfile serves as a site evaluation tool, providing profiles of geographic areas, household, and other demographic profiles.
- ClusterPlus provides detailed reporting on forty-seven distinct demographic clusters.
- ClusterPlus Workstation adds over 4,000 stored market definitions to the standard cluster analysis component; TargetScan serves to identify geographic locales that meet specific criteria and to draw maps of those areas in a number of detail levels.
- GraphicProfile provides advanced mapping capabilities. The software also includes several advanced features to import and export data, manage files, etc.

Del Mar Group

The Del Mar Group has an electronic shopping system called Retailer's Assistant that combines both CD-ROM technology and artificial intelligence (AI) software. The AI techniques clarify the customer's personal interests and tastes and then display the most appropriate products available for purchase. The customer first views a sequence of images, mostly those of products available in the store. Touching the product images informs the computer of individual likes and dislikes.

The program quickly zeroes in on individual preferences, displays products the customer may wish to purchase, suggests related items and accessories, and directs the user to the appropriate department or order desk. Retailer's Assistant can perform the following product information services: gift advice, personal shopping advice, product identification, presentation, promotion, demonstration, comparisons, location in the store, and market research.

Knowledge Access

Knowledge Access has consumer and business versions of Your Marketing Consultant which serves as a demographic analysis tool with thirty-nine consumer and thirty business-to-business variables. It covers 316 standard metropolitan statistical areas, 3,137 counties, and 423 other U.S. geographical units. It contains a complete set of on-screen state maps which the operator can display at three levels of magnification or 'zoom.' The KAware software permits addition of user data, output to spreadsheets, and report generation.

Knowledge Access also has the California Manufacturers' Directory, Selectory, and a subset of Microcomputer Index, known as MicroReviews, which contains abstracts of published hardware, software, and book reviews from forty-five source periodicals on microcomputing. A searcher may scan tables of contents or select from the menu to search by descriptor, document type, journal title, date, product and company, and rating. The Program Overview option provides an online tutorial and the user may download information. The company places no restrictions on the database's use other than a prohibition on reselling or widely redistributing the information use.

Infomark Laser PC System

National Decision Systems (NDS) has developed the Infomark Laser PC System which comes in both 12-inch videodisc and CD-ROM versions. The "mark" portion of the name stands for marketing. It includes six separate but integrated databases: 1) NDS demographic; 2) vision geo-demographic; 3) consumer expenditure, 4) site locator reference; 5) shopping center data, and 6) color mapping data.

This system meets the demands of retailers who are always looking for better, less expensive ways to obtain detailed demographic and real estate information. It is a self-contained, microcomputer-based system that provides an array of marketing data for nearly any location in the U.S.

Infomark includes complete latitude and longitude information as well as a color map for any U.S. area. It covers 85 million households, 48 market segments, and over 8,000 major shopping centers. The user can generate marketing information reports via zip codes, census tracts, states, counties, cities, or places. This product originally comes in optical format and has no corresponding print version.

Real Estate Data, Inc. has a tool for another type of business. The Real Estate Data: Washington DC Metro Area disc comprises the complete information about each parcel of property in the Washington, D.C. metropolitan area. It includes legal description, lot size, assessor's parcel number, owner's name and address, date of last sale and sale price, assessed value, and buyers' and sellers' names.

QuadVision

Quadram Corp. and Comsell have a video database system, known as QuadVision, which lets the user construct video databases and provide text and visual information for customers. The operator controls the data and the video through the PC and can also take the data off the CD-ROM for editing or transmission. QuadVision has a videodisc and CD-ROM players and the PC components built into a single unit which can serve up to eight PCs in a network environment.

The QuadVision system, directed at the wholesaling, manufacturing, and retailing markets, can facilitate electronic publication of manuals, catalogs, and support tools. Companies can also use it for re-order entry, training, point-of-sale order entry, and for organizing a database in text or in picture. Comsell provides the proprietary text and video databases and the premastering capabilities for the disc.

CD-Yellow Pages

Compact Discoveries has the *CD-Yellow Pages* which combines digitized images with supplementary information from multiple databases. The user accesses company names via subject headings. It also makes available additional information such as pictures, ads, store hours, credit cards, and maps on how to reach the business for each company. The disc also contains examples of digitized images. It can accommodate combined databases for use in catalog shopping, education, real estate, and emergency services.

Slater Hall's Products

Courtenay Slater, former chief economist for the U.S. Department of Commerce, and George Hall, former associate director of the Bureau of the Census, have joined forces in a company called Slater Hall Information Products (SHIP) to market economic and social statistics on CD-ROM. Their first disc contains the most recent Census of Agriculture. It covers more than 3,000 data items for each county in the country—items such as number of farms, sales of selected agricultural products, total agricultural sales, and changes in the counties from 1978 to 1982.

The company also has the 1929–1986 Business Indicators CD-ROM disc which contains three separate databases: complete GNP accounts from 1929 to 1986, business statistics, and income and employment figures by state and region. The business statistics file contains annual data from 1961 to 1985 and monthly data from 1981 to 1986.

It also has some 1,900 economic time series from the Commerce Department's "Blue Pages" in its monthly Survey of Current Business. It gives income and employment figures by state, with regional and national totals. This file includes some 450 time series. The disc uses Slater Hall's proprietary software called SEARCHER for information retrieval.

The company's most recent product, County Statistics, contains more than 1,200 items of statistical information about each U.S. county, state, and metropolitan area. It includes data from the Census Bureau's COSTAT2 tape plus additional data on population, employment, and agriculture as well as totals for all metropolitan statistical areas, consolidated metropolitan areas, and primary metropolitan statistical areas. The product covers twenty subject areas such as population, income, housing, health, education, business, agriculture, and crime statistics.

SHIP's subsequent discs will comprise such files as foreign trade statistics, employment statistics, personal income data, the census of U.S. manufacturers, resale and wholesale trade and services, and income and demographic data. The final selection will depend on the census bureau's update schedule and the timeliness of the data available. The U.S. Bureau of the Census has its own Census Test Disc which it is using to evaluate the feasibility of distributing the data from the next census in CD-ROM.

Supermap

Space-Time Research has produced a CD-ROM containing their own retrieval software, Supermap, and the 1981 Australian census figures. The 1986 census disc will follow the release of the data. Chadwyck-Healey, Inc. markets Supermap in the U.S. The American version includes the 1980 U.S. Census and digital mapping data on a single disc. The proprietary software lets the user retrieve, manipulate, tabulate, rank, scan, and map information in up to sixty-four colors or monochrome. It can accept user data and download to local software or data manipulators, such as Lotus 1-2-3. Step-by-step instructions appear on each screen for quick reference.

The operator extracts the data for mapping from retrieved tables, groups it into classes, and selects map colors and captions for each class. The system maps U.S. data onto prepared base maps for each state at the county level or for the whole country at the state level. The user can display the maps in a slow motion sequence that enables him or her to easily portray changes in data through a time sequence or to reflect comparative characteristics.

Tri-Star's Master Search

Tri-Star Publishing's Master Search, a trademark research system on CD-ROM has been delayed by litigation proceedings. Tri-Star hopes to release the product in late 1988. The four disc set provides the equivalent of all the records of the U.S. Patent and Trademark Office. It includes all available textual and image data for about 660,000 active trademarks and some not currently registered. The historical records comprise a three-disc set with a fourth monthly-updated disc containing the text and images of all new applications and all changes to records on the historical discs.

The Master Search system, which requires no formal training, lets each user make the system "remember" his or her own preferences. It provides very sophisticated searching capabilities in addition to being very easy to use. For example, wild card searching can locate prefixes, suffixes, and even letter sequences regardless of their position in a word; the synonym dictionary can identify trademarks with similar meanings; and the phonetic dictionary can serve to master fanciful spellings and word corruptions.

The operator can scan each resulting trademark very easily. The user controls the format and content of the text and graphics of the final screen display or reproduction from a printer. The searcher can also jot down any notes in the notebook to record any documentation of the trademark search. One can then transfer these annotations along with the chosen records to word processor packages for use in correspondence, legal opinions, or other uses.

Tri-Star also plans to release a patents CD-ROM product sometime during the year. The database will require six to eight drives to access all the discs.

Inventory Locator Service

Inventory Locator Service, Inc. (ILS) provides an extensive online cross-referenced aircraft/maritime parts database. It also has a CD-ROM version of its data. ILS's Integrated Logistics Service (ILOGS) combines a CD-ROM system with its 24-hour, 7-day per week online services. It currently processes over 40,000 part number inquiries per day from its 1,100 customers worldwide.

The initial CD-ROM disc contains the Master Cross-Reference List (MCRL), the Management List Consolidated (ML-C), and the Commercial and Government Entity (CAGE) databases. With the parts cross-referenced by manufacturer's part number, NSN number, MIL-Spec/MIL-Standard or drawing number, the operator can locate information on parts listed by Department of Defense (DOD) activities.

ILS plans a second disc to contain procurement history from seventeen DOD facilities, Technical Characteristics, the Next Higher

Assembly, the Master Repairable Item List (MRIL), the Master Index to Allowable Parts/Equipment List (MIAPL), and other data.

Automobile Parts Catalogs

Several other companies have also used CD-ROM to distribute parts catalogs for automobiles. ADP has Onsite Plus. Reynolds & Reynolds produced a Honda Parts Catalog disc and an Acura Parts Catalog. Bell & Howell's titles include Chrysler Parts Catalog, GM Parts Catalog, and Honda Parts Catalog.

Postal Applications

Information Design Incorporated (IDI) put the entire forty-seven-volume *National Postal Service Directory* on a single CD-ROM disc called the Address Verification System Plus (AVS+). It allows users to retrieve any U.S. address along with its ZIP+4 code in less than two seconds.

The information includes P.O. boxes, rural routes, named and numbered streets, apartment buildings, and firm names (corporations and professional people) for all of the U.S. and its trust territories. The disc also contains all the state lists of post offices, APO and FPO codes, building suite and floor numbers, cross-references, and alternate address codes.

In addition to retrieving address information, the system can serve to resolve discrepancies by identifying incomplete or incorrect addresses and validating new ones. As an operator keys in a new name and address, AVS+ can scan the National Directory and instantly display the address and ZIP+4 code on the screen for approval before transferral into the computer files, thus preventing incorrect or incomplete data from getting into the system.

AVS+ software can accommodate natural address entry by recognizing any format or any abbreviations currently in use. The split screen displays the entry fields on the left and the retrieved data on the right. The results resemble a page of the National Directory which the operator can scroll in both directions to browse and select the correct entry. The system can also check for spelling errors and provide phonetic matching.

ALDE Publishing also has the ZIP+4 Directory. Subscribers to

Microsoft's Bookshelf have access to the five-digit codes along with the other writer's tools contained on that disc.

British Postcode File

The British Post Office has a similar disc: the Postcode Address File. It lists some 23.5 million addresses and allows searching by any word in the name, street, or town fields or the postal code itself. It includes private and business names and addresses as well as links to the postal codes from Ordnance Survey grid reference data. For customers who want up-to-date, but not necessarily up-to-the-minute, information, the CD-ROM disc represents an ideal medium for identifying an address from keyed-in "partial" information in as little as two seconds—up to twenty times faster than with conventional paper methods. SilverPlatter's London office provides the search software and markets the disc.

Tetragon began shipping Business Base, the second disc in its "RAINBOW, The Connection" series, in early May, 1987. It contains 994,000 records on approximately 700,000 businesses throughout Canada. It indexes each Canadian firm by name, address, type of business, SIC code, telephone number and area code, postal code, city and province, and company description. It lists entries in both French and English. Tetragon president Charles De Matigny expects Business Base to outsell Home Base, the company's first disc, four to one.

Tax Information

Reference Technology, Inc. is working with Tax Analysts to put "Tax Notes Today" on a disc and has begun a pilot project to master and produce "Tax Court Opinions" from 1982 to the present (discussed later in the chapter).

Another area of CD-ROM product development is patent information. Nearly half a dozen companies, including International Computaprint Corp., Derwent, and Pergamon, already offer some form of patent information online; but they do not include images of the patent drawings. Several database producers are reportedly considering a laserdisc product with digitized images.

Medicine

The medical profession is another area that requires quick access to large quantities of information either online or in optical format.

Micromedex, Inc. created the Computerized Clinical Information System (CCIS), a medical information storage and retrieval system. It consists of four medical databases on CD-ROM which include:

1. Poisindex, a toxicology database that identifies and provides ingredient information on over 300,000 industrial, pharmaceutical, commercial, and botanical management/treatment protocols in the event of a toxic condition due to ingestion, absorption, or inhalation of any of the substances listed. It is indexed by manufacturer's name, brand/trade name, generic/chemical name, street/slang terminology, botanical name, and common name.
2. Drugdex, a pharmacologic database on over 3,700 investigational and foreign FDA-approved and OTC preparations.
3. Emergindex/Diagnostics and Therapeutics, a referenced clinical information system designed to present pertinent medical data for the practice of acute care medicine. It has a 40,000 keyword medical thesaurus.
4. Identidex/Tablet and Capsule Identification for identifying tablets and capsules by color and physical descriptions as well as by manufacturer imprint codes. The company provides yearly subscriptions to these databases with quarterly updates.

According to Micromedex, "the database search technique is geared to providing specific, evaluated answers to medical questions using a complex dictionary and index structure rather than free-text searching."

The National Library of Medicine (NLM) has signed several collaborative, experimental agreements to make it possible for commercial firms to market and distribute optical disk products containing MEDLARS data. The nonexclusive agreements cover approximately a one-year period. They permit licensees to choose any segment of MEDLINE to put on their discs or to offer MEDLINE records with other data with NLM's approval. All products will contain MEDLINE data at first; but we can assume that other MEDLARS databases will be added and marketed. During the first year, each licensee may promote, market, distribute, and sell the optical disk system containing MEDLARS data to either individuals or institutions at any price it deems reasonable.

BRS/Colleague Disc

BRS Information Technologies introduced the BRS/Colleague Disc, which contains only the English-language portion of MFDLINE beginning with January 1986 on two discs. Designed for medical students, researchers, physicians, and drug company professionals, it adapts the simple but powerful Colleague search software to the personal computer/CD-ROM environment and combines it with the most frequently used information in health care: MEDLINE. Its command and display formats resemble those of Colleague, BRS's online medical search service for health professionals.

MEDLINE Knowledge Finder

The Faxon Company has formed a strategic partnership with Aries Systems Corporation to distribute the MEDLINE Knowledge Finder which runs on the Apple Macintosh. It covers up to five years of MEDLINE drawn from all journals in the NLM's Abridged Index Medicus and in the Brandon/Hill journal lists recommended for small medical libraries, nursing, and allied health sciences. The disc includes the Medical Subject Headings (MeSH) thesaurus which has a seamless interface with the citation database permitting even novice searchers to use the MeSH vocabulary easily.

Knowledge Finder's software uses a probabilisitic bibliographic retrieval system that simplifies end-user searching while retaining the power and flexibility of traditional retrieval systems. It displays results in order of their likely relevance to the search statement, thereby reducing the amount of time the searcher spends reviewing search results.

One can order several MEDLINE database subsets with Knowledge Finder. The Core Journal Subset includes 250,000 citations, many with abstracts, to articles published in 220 journals during the current year and four previous years. An unabridged MEDLINE scheduled to appear in mid-1988 will contain all MEDLINE titles, including both English and foreign language publications. The data for each year will come on a separate disc with coverage offered for the current year and the five most recent backfile years.

As already mentioned, MEDLINE will appear as the second offering of DIALOG OnDisc as well as in OCLC's Search CD450 family.

CL-MEDLINE

CLSI, Inc.'s version of MEDLINE, called CL-MEDLINE, comes on a 12-

inch WORM disc. It contains four years of the MEDLINE database with journal citations and full MeSH references. It can support six to twelve users locally or as a server for remote terminals.

Digital Diagnostics has a variation of the MEDLINE database known as BiblioMed. Designed for the practicing physician, it has an easy to learn and use search system. Rather than include all articles from MEDLINE, company executives decided to have physicians at Johns Hopkins and the Mayo Clinic select specific articles for inclusion based on their usefulness to a practicing doctor.

Cambridge Scientific Abstracts includes the Life Sciences Collection as well as MEDLINE as part of Compact Cambridge, a series of databases produced by Cambridge and other suppliers. (It also includes the Aquatic Sciences & Fisheries Abstracts [ASFA] database which includes over 110,000 abstracts.) Cambridge hopes to acquire additional databases over the long term and has approached several producers with an eye to cooperative CD-ROM ventures.

CD/Biotech

The International Association for Scientific Computing (IASC) produces CD/Biotech as the first offering in its Megazines series. It comprises a collection of biotechnology databases and journal articles from:

1. Genbank (the NIH [National Institutes of Health]-sponsored Genetic Sequences Databank) in both complete and condensed format.
2. The National Biomedical Research Foundation's Protein Identification Resource (complete and condensed).
3. The European Molecular Biology Laboratory's Data Library.

It also contains several hundred operational programs of interest to scientists.

Researchers using CD/Biotech can locate technical papers simply by typing keywords. A listing of relevant titles appears within seconds. The operator can then access the abstracts or even the original paper. IASC plans to release more Megazines applicable to other scientific and engineering disciplines.

University Microfilms International (UMI) Article Clearinghouse has been selected as one of two document distribution centers in the United States for the ADONIS CD-ROM Biomedical Collection which consists of 219 frequently requested biomedical journals, predominantly published by the members of the ADONIS consortium: Blackwell Scientific Publications, Ltd. and Springer-Verlag GmbH.

Six other publishers contributed titles to the project as well: Butterworth Scientific, Ltd., Churchill Livingstone, the C.V. Mosby Company, Munksgaard International Publishers, Ltd., Georg Thieme Verlag, and John Wiley and Sons, Ltd. With storage space becoming more and more of a problem in libraries, the ADONIS project will publish text and graphics of over 200 medical journals on weekly CD-ROM discs.

During the two-year pilot program, users can order photocopies of full-text articles through the Clearinghouse. Copies will be produced on a high-resolution laser printer and sent to the user within 24 hours via mail, telefacsimile, or overnight courier. New discs will arrive at the Clearinghouse each week to ensure the timeliness of the information.

Faxon's Document Delivery Service

The Faxon Company introduced its Biomedical Document Delivery Service (BDDS) for users of its Infoserv online service. It provides hard copy delivery of articles from some 219 scientific, technical, and medical journals selected because of their inclusion in the ADONIS database. Faxon intends to ship requested articles the same day via Information on Demand, Inc. at a cost of $10 per article.

Another European endeavor, Medata-Rom, involves Telesystemes, as project leader, together with CNRS and Inserm (France) and Excerpta Medica (Netherlands). The group will produce a CD-ROM every two months which will contain monthly updates of three major medical databases: MEDLINE, Embase, and Pascal. Questel Plus software will permit searching in both English and French.

Bio-ROM

Questel software will be extended to handle graphics in another joint enterprise, Bio-ROM, in a collaboration led by Derwent Publications. This will cover biotechnology patent abstracts and journal literature. A project called BIOREP under the leadership of the Dutch research organization ZWO will make available online information regarding biotechnology research projects.

The National Institute of Occupational Safety and Health (NIOSH) has produced an optical version of the *Registry of Toxic Effects of Chemical Substances* (RTECS) which SilverPlatter markets (see the Abstracts and Indexes section in Chapter 5).

CCINFO CD-ROMs

The Canadian Centre for Occupational Health and Safety has two series in its CCINFO CD-ROM line. Series A includes:

- Tradenames, a listing of more than 29,000 manufactured chemicals and corresponding precautions.
- Cheminfo, a database of approximately 650 pure chemicals, natural substances, and mixtures used in or resulting from industrial processes.
- Registry of Toxic Effects of Chemical Substances (RTECS), a source of worldwide toxicity data for more than 88,000 chemicals.
- Transportation of Dangerous Goods, a database of Canadian and international regulations concerning chemical shipping by rail, road, and sea.
- Regulatory Information on Pesticide Products (RIPP), a file of more than 7,000 pesticides registered in Canada under the Pest Control Products Act. It includes agricultural forestry pesticides, wood preservatives, home and garden pesticides, and industrial slimicides. Each entry lists the ingredients, concentration, mode of application, intended pest to control, and locations considered safe for application (i.e., near food, livestock, people, etc.).

CCINFO-Series B contains additional data on occupational health and safety. It includes NIOSHTIC, a bibliographic file of worldwide literature organized by the U.S. National Institute for Occupational Safety and Health. It also comprises CANADIANA which contains annotated references to occupational health and safety documents published in Canada.

Other products include the I.S. Group's Oncodisc, Medical Economics Company's PDR Direct Access, and MicroTrends, Inc.'s BioLibe.

Law

The legal community is another large market for CD-ROM information products. Some companies like UTLAS with LAWMARC have produced databases of bibliographic records to facilitate cataloging and identifying legal materials. Information Access Company markets LegalTrac as an add-on to its InfoTrac system on videodisc. It indexes 500,000 articles from over 730 law journals, newspapers, and other legal publications. Indexing begins with January 1982. Other companies are concentrating on the legal documents themselves.

Wang, Inc. and West Publishing Co. announced that they will work together to provide CD-ROM products and systems for the legal community. West has the full text of its WESTLAW database available online while Wang has a large market share of the installed base of equipment currently installed in law offices.

The Michie Company has the Code of the Commonwealth of Virginia on CD-ROM. Presently, this is the only state code in this format. Michie is also considering the state code of Hawaii as a likely candidate because it is the only state that doesn't have its laws on some online service. The data, however, is in machine-readable form at a large electronic publishing concern in California; and it would be relatively easy to transfer the data to disc.

PHINet Tax Resources

Prentice-Hall produces the PHINet tax resource library. It includes 490 megabytes (MB) of data covering regulations, cases, rulings, letter rulings, and administrative interpretations that make up the critical body of tax law. Reference Technology, Inc. mastered the disc which uses their search software.

In addition to the Prentice-Hall product, tax lawyers and accountants have CD-ROM access to nearly one gigabyte of primary tax material including code, legislative histories, private letter rulings, and court decisions. Tax Analysts, which publishes *Tax Notes Today* in print and electronic form, has created the CD-ROM product as part of a proposal to the Internal Revenue Service. The main source material fills seven discs. An eighth disc updates the collection on a quarterly basis while online service provides access to changes since the last update. The IRS is currently evaluating the discs and CD-ROM technology as a way to control research costs, which the agency says are now "out of control." On the other hand, Eurolex has a disc of European case law available.

Online Computer Systems, Inc. planned to market a package of federal and state income tax forms on CD-ROM. This would be the first product in a series of demand publishing products they expected to undertake.

U.S. Code of Federal Regulations

TMS (Time Management Software) of Stillwater, Oklahoma, has three titles of the U.S. Code of Federal Regulations on CD-ROM discs (TMS Research). The company uses them to demonstrate how TMS search software handles large full-text databases such as the Internal Revenue Code, the Social Security Database, and the Public Health Code. Although TMS which is a data-preparation and search-software firm has no plans to sell the discs, it would be pleased if they attracted clients who want to sell the entire code on disc.

Quantum Access, Inc. compiles state and federal regulations on CD-ROM for specific vertical markets such as education and the oil and gas industry. Their first product, the State Education Encyclopedia, contains all the legislative and regulatory material that a Texas school administrator might need: state legislation, policies and procedures of the Texas Education Agency, curriculum guides, transcripts of administrative hearings, court cases, and state interpretations of administrative hearings. Previously, most of this information could only be retrieved by searching through the Texas Education Agency archives.

Quantum's second offering, the Texas Attorney General Documents, contains the full text of the documents from the Texas Attorney General's Office from 1979 to 1986. Updates include new decisions and important historical rulings dating back to 1949. They also include the Open Records Act Decisions, letter advisories, and constitutional convention advisories.

Some of Quantum's other products in development include: oil and gas data on drilling, production, and transportation; and technical data, repair manuals, and parts catalogs for equipment used in oil and gas production. It is also working on the development of proprietary software for each of its products.

Mead Data Central is conducting focus groups and market tests that should culminate in several CD-ROM products for the legal and accounting markets.

Government

ALDE Publishing has several products providing full-text access to selected government publications. The Federal Acquisition/Procurement Disc (Title 41/48) covers Title 41/48 dealing with U.S. Government acquisition and procurement issues. The Title 20 USC/CFR disc covers

Title 20, Social Security, while the Title 26 USC/CFR disc deals with Title 26, Internal Revenue code and regulations and the Title 42 USC/CFR disc deals with Title 42, Public Health Code and Health and Human Services Regulations.

All the databases include material from the *U.S. Code* and the *Code of Federal Regulations*. ALDE also has the Zip+4 Directory which includes the complete national ZIP+4 directory provided by the U.S. Post Office. All of these databases are available in both CD-ROM and videodisc formats.

In addition, ALDE publishes USSR Source 21, a Soviet reference library which contains 30MB of Soviet designed software, the complete *Communist Manifesto,* gross economic indicators since 1960, descriptions of space launches and payloads, technical information on weapons systems since 1965, USSR almanac/world records, cartographic information, transcripts of Academy of Science annual meetings, *Pravda,* Izvestia, TASS, organizational charts of agencies such as the KGB, and biographies of politburo members since 1912.

ALDE also plans to publish about eight other foreign national databases which will contain material gathered from public domain data collections available from sources in the U.S. and the other country, from publishers with specific country information willing to work with ALDE on a royalty basis, and other content potential users consider important, as determined by a series of focus groups ALDE will conduct.

VLS's CD-ROMs

VLS, Inc. produced the Code of Federal Regulations on CD-ROM which includes the complete Code, Titles 1–50. Its product identification scheme is a little confusing, partly due to the eccentric manner in which the GPO releases the data. OPTEXT Issue No. 101 comprises two volumes (discs). Volume One contains titles 28–41, with data current as of July 1, 1986. Volume Two contains titles 42–50, current as of October 1, 1985. Issue No. 103 (VLS decided not to make these numbers consecutive) also consists of two volumes comprising titles 1–16 (current as of January 1, 1986) and titles 17–27 (current as of April 1, 1986).

A unique VLS service, OPTEXT Online Demo, lets a user dial-up to use and evaluate the CD-ROM database. The company also plans a disc series which will contain the five previous quarters of the *Federal Register*. It will have quarterly updates with the oldest months falling off with each issue. The initial subscription fee for the entire package includes these four editions.

Environmental Resources Management (ERM) Computer Services, Inc. has developed ENFLEX INFO which provides an updated compilation of the full text of all federal and state environmental regulations. ERM staff organize and index the information to meet compliance, monitoring, permits, and reporting requirements.

The National Standards Association has produced its parts catalog under the title Parts Master for providers of products and services to the U.S. military and government purchasing departments. The product, based on the National Stock Number System, shows how to correlate component identification in any of the systems used throughout the government to buy material.

It gives complete information about the requirements of each of the 12 million parts acquired by the government: shape, size, packaging, ratings, test data, etc. Some of the features include: NSN, FSC, FSCM, NSCM, IL's (Technical Characteristics), FSCNM, Military Part Numbers, and a few dozen other data fields and classes. It comprises three discs; but the company claims it is so easy to use that the documentation covers less than thirty pages.

"Norwegian Domesday Book"

Archetype Systems has produced a 50MB CD-ROM database giving population statistics from 1976–1986 and projections to 2011 for all 454 Norwegian municipalities. It includes maps and satellite data as well as an encyclopedia supplement covering local and current international affairs. The project aims to facilitate town and country planning and is seen as a prototype for a "Norwegian Domesday Book."

Department of Defense

Since the DOD directed that all military installations must be self-contained in case of nuclear attack, NASA has selected CD-ROM systems for storing technical manuals for the planned orbiting space station. This would save a great deal of space and weight aboard the craft.

For the same reason, the U.S. Navy decided to put its technical and maintenance manuals for the Trident submarine's on-board systems onto

CD-ROM discs. A Trident's mission often calls for long periods of time without communication and any equipment problem must be solved on the sub and very little space is available for storing the lengthy technical material that goes with the sophisticated gear.

NASA's Jet Propulsion Laboratory (JPL) selected CD-ROM for storing space images on earth. The data from the space exploration missions, such as Voyager's fly-by of the moons of Jupiter and Uranus, are transmitted to NASA from satellites and stored on magnetic tape. The tapes are available to researchers all over the world.

Since one mission, however, can generate 250 tapes, accessing the data and maintaining the tapes can present problems. CD-ROM offers a solution that is easy to distribute and will not deteriorate with age. JPL has already produced one prototype disc with Voyager images and a larger project is expected to begin shortly.

Education

Several academic centers are working on laser optic projects for use in education. Some of these include the Shakespeare project on interactive videodisc at Stanford University, the Dante project at Dartmouth, and Cornell University's English department's disc on Black Fiction to 1920. The University of California at Irvine is working on the *Thesaurus Linguae Graecae* while Harvard University Press continues its work on the Loeb classics.

In the commercial area, Ibycus Systems developed the Scholarly Personal Computer, a specially-designed workstation to support students and scholars working with ancient Greek, Latin, Hebrew, and Coptic literature. The computer is equipped with a CD-ROM drive and uses a disc that contains the works of ancient Greek authors such as Homer, Sophocles, Plato, Aristotle, and Plutarch. It also contains the Greek New Testament, the Hebrew and Greek versions of the Old Testament, and the works of a number of Coptic and Latin authors, including Virgil.

Tri-Star Publishing plans to produce CD-ROMs for the law and education markets. It expects to release the complete works of Shakespeare some time in 1988. Several of its projects will provide educational research products targeted to university libraries. However, since the company is still negotiating these products, it has not released any further details.

Interage Research, Inc. developed a world history software program called Fast Past. It contains 5,000 articles describing historic events and people from 10,000 B.C. to the present. It tries to create the sensation of time travel. The floppy disk version sells for $135 by mail order. The CD-ROM version includes graphics and audio.

Fast Past by MicroTrends

MicroTrends, Inc. has a product called Fast Past. It also produces the LinguaTech Bilingual Dictionary, Menu, Nature Plus, and Versa Text. U.S. West Knowledge Engineering is working on the College Blue Book.

PC-SIG, Inc. released the Science Helper K–8 which contains almost 1,000 science and mathematics lesson plans for kindergarten through eighth grade. They emphasize process skills and require inexpensive materials.

The software allows searching the lesson plan titles on any combination of criteria: grade level, academic subject, curriculum project, words or phrases, science processes, or content themes. All these public-domain documents contain teacher-written abstracts which can be freely copied and distributed.

Tescor, Inc. and Reference Technology are collaborating on CD-ROM products and services associated with the First National Item Bank and Test Development System. Tescor developed the project to enable elementary and secondary school districts to set up complete in-house programs to author, produce, and score quality test instruments. Educators can now choose from among tens of thousands of test items already used by their colleagues to test mastery of thousands of state and local curricular objectives.

Intechnica Learning Systems, Inc. demonstrated a series of CD-ROMs which teach users foreign languages using natural sounding speech for vocal practice and tutorials for reinforcement. The system configuration requires a special VoxCard for the computer and a CD-ROM drive with audio capabilities. The software accommodates networking and includes a record-keeping unit to monitor each student's progress.

Apple Computer, Inc. has signed an agreement with the National Geographic Society and Lucasfilm, Ltd. which will permit the company to investigate applications for optical technologies in education. It hopes to develop videodiscs, compact discs, and CD-ROMs to provide students and educators with more control over information, whether text, graphics, or still or moving pictures. While the company's plans remain in the developmental stage, a spokesperson indicates it will focus more on imaging and video than on CD-ROMs.

Science

While many scientific applications will use WORM technology to store and distribute engineering drawings and similar materials, several publishers have found CD-ROM appropriate for their information products. McGraw-Hill Book Company's Science and Technical Reference Set has been discussed in the Reference Works section of Chapter 5.

The Institute for Scientific Information (ISI) released a CD-ROM edition of *Science Citation Index* (SCI), the world's largest interdisciplinary science index in May, 1988 under the title Science Citation Index Compact Disc Edition (SCI CD). The print version consists of four separate but related indexes (Citation Index, Permuterm Subject Index, Source Index, and Corporate Index); but the CD-ROM covers only the Permuterm Subject Index with work underway for a prototype of the Citation Index.

SCI CD provides a variety of options throughout the search process. Operators can select items to define a search by browsing through "dictionaries" of cited authors, works, or patents; title words; author name or address; and journal titles. They can move between dictionaries to choose qualifying search terms or they can bypass the dictionaries by directly keying in their search strategy. The system supports Boolean logic and truncation within and across dictionaries and permits saving and reusing search statements.

Once the user has identified some useful papers, SCI CD's "related records" feature enables him or her to find other relevant material quickly and easily. It uses hypertext software to retrieve related articles through the links the authors create when their bibliographies have references in common. When it locates an item, it can list up to twenty related records.

It also shows the total number of shared references upon retrieving each related record. These shared references provide the key to establishing a relationship between the articles. Even though the two articles may have no title words in common, SCI CD can still establish a subject relationship using the shared references.

The set includes two self-contained and independently searchable CD-ROMs, each with its own unique entry points and features, quarterly cumulative updates, search and retrieval software with context-sensitive help, user documentation, an annual archival cumulation, and a toll-free help number.

John Wiley CD-ROMs

John Wiley & Sons introduced three CD-ROM products. The Kirk–Othmer Encyclopedia of Chemical Technology, Wiley's standard reference work on chemistry and the chemical industry, includes the entire contents of the 24-volume printed work—nearly 1,200 articles plus index and supplements.

The Mark Encyclopedia of Polymer Science and Engineering focuses on applied polymer and plastics technology. Eleven volumes of the nineteen-volume work have already appeared. Wiley plans to release four volumes each calendar year through 1989. Purchasers of the CD-ROM edition will receive the current discs immediately along with annual updates until completion.

Wiley also has a CD-ROM version of the *International Dictionary of Medicine and Biology*, the largest medical dictionary available in English. The printed edition covers three printed volumes and defines more than 160,000 terms.

The publisher previously released the *1987 Registry of Mass Spectral Data* which includes the spectra and supports search access of the database's extensive chemical name and synonym files which also include nearly 90,000 CAS Registry Numbers.

Cambridge Scientific Abstracts' Pollution/Ecology/Toxicology CD-ROM includes 7,150 abstracts with subject/author indexes in toxicology per year, 9,600 in ecology, and 9,000 in pollution. The software allows menu- or command-driven access to search by author, title, subject, keyword, or phrase with proximity.

Powder Diffraction File

The International Centre for Diffraction Data produced its Powder

Diffraction File on CD-ROM. It serves to identify unknown compounds, specifically those in crystalline or a solid state. It contains 120MB of data covering 48,000 different compounds indexed by chemical name, mineral name, chemical constituents, D-spacings, file identification number, powder diffraction number, etc. Reference Technology, the firm preparing the disc, also markets and distributes it.

PCI, Inc. produces the Resors database in CD-ROM. The Canada Centre for Remote Sensing (CCRS) assembles and maintains it online and, together with the Canadian Federal Department of Energy Mines and Resources, licenses it to PCI. Resors contains references to journal articles, reports, and symposia in English and French. It includes more than 53,000 items accessible by category, keywords, author, author affiliations, publication, and publication date.

Questel software and the British Library are working on a CD-ROM version of an encyclopedic work of chemistry comprising heterocyclic, organometallic, polymer, and coordination chemistry. Each component normally takes up 10,000 pages in an expensive printed form. The disc version will provide menu access in English, French, and German and accommodate chemical structure and full-text searching as well as analyses of contents.

U.S. WEST Knowledge Engineering and WBLA, Inc. have introduced Hydrodata, a software package designed to meet the water-data needs of professionals in the water resource field. It uses CD-ROM to publish the U.S. Geological Service Daily Values for the western states. It includes more than 100 years of river flow, water quality, and lake measurements.

Inacom International demonstrated a system that integrates an engineering database management system (DBMS) program and CD-ROM database using Reference Technology's CLASIX system. Design engineers use Parametrix, a DBMS program, to identify information, including diagrams and data sheets, about integrated and semiconductor circuits. The Tech-Doc/Digital Data laserbase comprises a set of engineering and manufacturer data books on CD-ROM. A special feature of the system allows the engineer to use the CD-ROM disc as if turning pages in a data book.

The National Institute of Builders produced a couple of discs for its constituents under the titles Building Sciences Information and Engineering Information Systems. The National Safety Data Corp. mastered the Material Safety Data Sheets. Quantum has a similar disc title: Material Safety Data System and Innovative Technology has the Technical Logistics Reference Network.

Information Handling Services has a database of some ten million pages of military specifications, industry standards, and vendor catalogs. Although it has most of them on microfiche, it mastered its index on CD-ROM, under the title CrossLink, with the view of eventually putting the entire product line on disc. The system allows an engineer or product designer to specify a product, search for the appropriate standards and for all the vendors whose products meet the specifications prior to selecting a particular item for use.

Geographic Applications

Map and geographic information is rather difficult and time consuming to update and produce in traditional paper formats. Yet, some groups and firms like land developers, political organizations, municipal and public utilities, and tax offices, among others, rely on it regularly and heavily. Geovision, Inc. is creating a library of maps and other types of graphic and geographic information on CD-ROM to meet their needs. Its GEOdisc represents a family of products that contains basic map images and related data of the continental U.S. based on satellite images and data from a multitude of government agencies. This includes vector and raster data, maps from many sources: USGS (digital line graphs and digital elevation models), NOAA, EOSAT (Landsat), Census Bureau, etc. The set comes in four series: National, Regional, State, and Metro.

Geovision aims to develop a complete PC-based geographic information system that allows periodic refreshment of data and permits the user to create, store, and maintain facility, boundary, or engineering records and graphics in an independent but totally compatible database. Its proprietary applications program, called Windows/On The World, runs in the Microsoft "Windows" environment and permits the exchange of data between that retrieved from the GEOdisc and other applications like word processors. Output is compatible with several major graphics packages, including Halo (Media Cybernetics) and Autocad (Autodesk, Inc.).

The company also provides the Georgia state disc, the first in its state mapping series. It contains ten times the detail of the national mapping disc and a greater number of data sets. It includes graphic information on Georgia's highways, roads and trails, rivers, streams and creeks, pipelines, power transmission lines, county boundaries, census tracts, and other features. In addition to retrieving information, users can display it and manipulate it using the Windows/On the World software. The second state disc will cover Florida.

Virginia Polytechnic Institute

The Cooperative Library Services Program at the Virginia Polytechnic Institute and State University (VPI) has received funding or in-kind support from a variety of institutions and businesses throughout the Commonwealth of Virginia to produce The Virginia Disc: An Evaluation of Locally Produced CD-ROM Products.

The project should result in 100 copies of two CD-ROMs, containing such data as 20MB of the Virginiana Collection from the Virginia State Library's historical bibliographic records, 60MB of VPI Library's MARC coded records of serial publications, 10MB of the InterAmerican Compendium of Registered Veterinary Drug Products with a demonstration of advanced retrieval methods for veterinary medical databases, the Virginia VIEW database of 6,000 pages of job and career opportunities in Virginia, the Virginia State Civil Engineering Survey database, full text of all publications from the Virginia Technical Extension Division, and more such state-related information.

The United States Geological Survey has awarded a contract to TMS to develop a prototype CD-ROM/microcomputer system that will store earth science and geological information, LANDSAT images, and general management documents.

DeLorme Global Mapper

DeLorme Mapping Systems has a world atlas on CD-ROM. The DeLorme Global Mapper contains information on political boundaries, roads, cities, and other place names, rivers, lakes, islands, land elevations, and worldwide ocean depths. It also includes examples of many types of government database information such as Census Bureau street maps and U.S. Geological Survey digital maps. This basic data can be customized to meet individual users' needs by the creation of overlays.

The first screen displays a general map of the world. The user moves the cursor over the area of interest and presses the mouse button to get more detail. The location of the last mouse click becomes the new map center, thus allowing the user to make lateral location adjustments when zooming in. The system has sixteen levels of zoom. At each level down, the scale halves and the amount of detail increases four-fold. At the most detailed scale, the monitor displays an area of the world one-half mile square.

DeLorme sees its potential market as trucking companies, shipping companies, railroads, utilities, police, fire and ambulance operations, and government agencies that have mobile operations. Such customers could use digital maps along with DeLorme's Fleet Management System Software to keep track of the location of all their vehicles.

A delivery company dispatcher, for example, could type in the name of a customer who has requested a pick-up and the system would highlight the customer's location on the PC screen along with the location of trucks in the customer's vicinity. The dispatcher could then determine which vehicle to assign to the pick-up.

The relative ease of updating digital maps (as opposed to conventional paper maps which can take months or years to update) is more than merely a nice feature. In addition to these products, Highlighted Data has a product called The Map Cabinet.

Hitachi's Personal Mapping System

Hitachi developed the Personal Mapping System, or P-Map, for map construction. It utilizes maps of government boundaries, railways, roadways, and buildings to construct customized maps which may be cross-indexed. Each CD-ROM has a capacity to store about 500 districts. The market for the product includes users in real estate, utilities, transportation, public services, and research and marketing areas.

CARIN (Car Information and Navigation) is the first motor vehicle CD-ROM-computer-based information and navigational system. It uses both data CD-ROMs and entertainment CDs. It is in operation in the Netherlands and Japan; but it does not seem likely that it will come to the U.S. market before 1990 when the last of the navigational satellites should be in place. The system uses the satellites to locate the car's present position, then refers to maps stored on the CD-ROM and a viewer to plot a course.

Designers expect it to reduce fuel consumption, decrease travel time and mileage, and continuously link the driver to car functions and road and weather conditions. With the driver's intended destination entered into an on-board computer, the system compares road information on a CD-ROM with the car's actual speed and route using a method of 'dead reckoning' which is an intermediate solution until it can use the more accurate Navstar Global Positioning System.

A speech synthesis unit gives the driver route information and provides instructions for correction if he or she deviates or makes a wrong turn. Further refinements include the use of the European Radio Data System which broadcasts digital traffic information which CARIN can use to revise a route to take road work or traffic jams into account. Its cost will vary depending upon the functions required, such as a link to the fuel system that warns the driver and provides a route to the nearest refueling point.

Geographic Data Technology, Inc. developed a CD-ROM map information storage and retrieval system for vehicle navigation systems. The system requires a 256K personal computer and shares an entertainment CD player wired into the vehicle. The firm envisions digitally encoded street maps stored on CD-ROM as having both static and mobile uses. N.V. Philips and Chrysler have also proposed using compact disc players in automobiles for both in-car entertainment and information.

The maps include all streets and sufficient house number and intersection information indexed to permit locating a precise street address or a street intersection. Additional useful information includes flagging one-way streets and turn restrictions as well as identifying highways and major arteries. These additions permit highlighting of expressways on the map display.

Rather than publishing national maps in this format, the company believes that it makes more sense to publish regional or state discs supplemented with a wealth of information targeted for specific markets. These could include applications directed to various public utilities and services as well as government for:

- Automated dispatching of taxicabs by pre-encoded geographic zones, thus reducing the possibility of favoritism on the part of the dispatcher.
- Sales territory alignment and sales call planning.

- Routing delivery and pick-up vehicles.
- Modeling postal carrier routes for zip code and carrier route realignment.
- Assignment and sequencing of service calls by plumbers and other repair/maintenance personnel.

Mitsubishi Electric Corp. and Japan Radio Co. have jointly developed a satellite navigation system that can pinpoint a car's location on a map with an accuracy of 100 meters. The system consists of a CD-ROM, Global Positioning Satellite (GPS) receiver, 13-centimeter flat antenna, and 6-inch color monitor. It should appear commercially in 1989 at a cost of more than $1,500.

Historical Weather Data

Of the several gigabytes of data that the National Oceanic and Atmospheric Administration (NOAA) downloads every day, it has selected some historical weather data for storage on a prototype CD-ROM disc to evaluate its usefulness as a reference and teaching tool. NOAA's largest database, the data from the Landsat satellite, might be a candidate for storage and distribution in this format.

As various petroleum and timber companies use the imagery in mapping activities and for prospecting, there is already a large market for the Landsat data. Transfer of the database from tape to disc could simplify distribution.

Lasertrak Corporation developed Lasertrak Pathfinder, a unique product intended to provide pilots with navigation charts and map data for filing alternate flight plans and related tasks. A proprietary computer operates from cockpit power sources in flight to read the information. The company plans to provide complete information service to pilots and navigators, including directories and other databases.

Miscellaneous

Data Base Products, Inc. produced O&D Plus, the first aviation information database on CD-ROM. It consists of three discs based on the Department of Transportation's Origin and Destination (O&D) Survey. They include statistical tables from the survey integrated with fare and yield numbers, passenger counts, average passenger revenue,

revenue by passenger mile, and more. The data covers approximately 120 air carriers and 1,084 domestic U.S. locations.

Volume I, the archival disc, contains seven years (1979-1985) of detailed quarterly origin and destination data with fares and yield numbers. Volume II contains two complete years of quarterly information up to the most current quarter. Volume III concentrates on itineraries provided with Table 12 of the O&D survey as well as fares and yield numbers. Recent additions to the series include Onboard and International.

BBC Domesday Project

The most ambitious CD-ROM project yet undertaken is the BBC Domesday Project intended to portray life as it exists in Great Britain in 1986 through the use of moving and still pictures, sounds, and text.

RTI (Reference Technology, Inc.) also has a subcontract from Electronic Data Systems for a field delivery system for the U.S. Department of Customs. The project will store 2,000 features of the faces of missing children as an aid to identification.

Public Domain Software

PC-SIG has the PC-SIG Library on CD-ROM. The Library Corporation has a similar product under the label PC Laser Library. The software library includes programs and documentation from the PC-SIG (Personal Computer Software Interest Group) library of public domain and user supplied software.

It includes a broad selection of programs for word processing, editing, database management, statistical analysis, programming languages, and printer utilities. Digital Decus Group has two software discs for the VAX family of computers called DECUS: Fall 1986 and DECUS: Spring 1987.

Blue Sail Software, Inc. recently announced an agreement with ALDE Publishing Co. to make its 1,000-diskette public domain software library available on CD-ROM for use with the IBM PC/XT/AT and compatibles. The disc contains over 3,000 programs and utilities compiled from the archives of several PC bulletin boards and from the cooperation of shareware authors.

ALDE uses the traditional microcomputer marketing model for distribution and sales of its CD-ROM products. Blue Sail and ALDE expect to announce shortly another agreement to make a CD-ROM disc of public domain software on a selected subject available each month.

Multi-Ad Services, Inc. developed the Kwikee INHOUSE Graphic Services disc for the Apple Macintosh. It contains high-quality vector-graphics art for desktop publishing. The software allows manipulating the art and including it and any text into a layout program.

Full-Text Newspapers

Datatek Corp. developed a system to store newspaper data in CD-ROM format. It will publish the full text of ten newspapers as well as newswires and databases which its DataTimes service offers online. Thus, it will be able to compress about three years of daily newspaper production onto one side of a disc.

The company will use the system in-house at first to replace tape storage of archival data. It will allow publishers to develop easily accessible discs of information, distribute them, and provide data to their reporters, librarians, and online customers. Later, it may market it to the public.

Other newspapers have explored mastering their editions on CD-ROM. Info Globe produced the Globe and Mail as an experimental product for the *Toronto Globe and Mail*. Data Times also produced the *Daily Oklahoman* on CD-ROM.

Teleflora's CD-ROM

Teleflora, a national network of more than 18,000 florists, uses CD-ROM technology to help subscribers speed deliveries and analyze services. Its DoveSystem includes an 1,800-page directory of subscribers as well as personalized information on how much floral wire service business the shops generate.

Florists can quickly locate other members by zip code or by city and state. They can determine prices of floral arrangements and plants, locate special products, and select the best shop geographically to fill the order. Then, the DoveSystem automatically dials the selected shop and places the order.

CineScan

Jonathan Pollard has developed a CD-ROM of newsreel summaries for the years 1929 to 1967, called CineScan (formerly NewScan). One part contains the International Newsreel Collection (1919–1984) formerly The American Newsreel Collection, a compilation of newsreel summaries from the archives of several production companies.

CineScan includes Hearst News of the Day (1910–1967), Hearst Farm Newsreel (1958), This Week in Sports (1954–1963), Hearst Telenews Weekly (1954–1963), Hearst Almanac, Hearst Reports, Time Out for Sports, Great Moments in Sports, Perspectives in Greatness, and the King Features Time Capsule, all from Hearst Metrotone News (NYC). The March of Time (1935–1950) from SFM Media Corporation and Paramount Newsreels (1927–1957) from the Sherman Grindberg Library, both in New York, also form part of this collection as does British Pathe, 1894–1970.

The disc also indexes the NASA film/video productions organized by the Lyndon B. Johnson Space Center in Houston. Its records range from the assembly and fabrication of the Mercury spacecraft in 1960 to the disastrous flight of the Space Shuttle Columbia in 1986.

CineScan consists of a full-text database that includes a single index covering every word. To identify particular film segments, the user just enters the terms that best describe the topic, examines the abstracts, retrieves the summaries, records the appropriate library location(s), and picks up the phone or writes a letter to the holding library. ABC's Newsreels and Footage '88, an independent film and tape sourcebook, also provides information about film availability across the country. Mr. Pollard has also expressed interest in developing CD-ROM discs which contain text and full images of collections from small art museums.

LaserData announced its LaserView turnkey system that stores, retrieves, and distributes electronic pages. It is available in two configurations: one for electronic filing and the other for electronic publishing. It is expected to serve as an electronic storage device for printed documents or microfilm and is intended as an online central data storage site with an image scanner for data input, a personal computer-based workstation, and a laser printer and WORM drive for data distribution.

The workstation can serve to maintain documents which incorporate text and images onto WORM discs. Typical applications include technical documentation, bank records, and customer files.

The electronic publishing configuration includes a workstation, a laser printer, and a CD-ROM drive or network to support distribution across multiple sites. Potential applications of this configuration include parts catalogs, journals, magazines, and corporate publications.

Continuous Information Service

IDG Communications introduced its CD-ROM Continuous Information Service (CIS) to provide an independent source for the evaluation of CD-ROM products. It provides clients with the *CD-ROM Lab Report,* the *IDG Report on CD-ROM, CD-ROM Review,* and personal access to the CD-ROM Lab and the CIS staff.

The CD-ROM Lab, established in January, 1988, conducts extensive compatibility and usability tests. It is equipped with all major types of microcomputers, including an IBM PC AT, IBM PS/2, major MS-DOS clones, and a Macintosh, as well as CD-ROM drives from every major manufacturer worldwide. Clients may schedule a visit to talk with lab technicians, test their discs, and observe the tests in process.

The *CD-ROM Lab Report* reviews and analyzes between twenty-five and thirty major CD-ROM products per quarter. Authorities in the respective fields use rigorous lab testing as their basis.

The *IDG Report on CD-ROM* is a monthly insiders' report on the latest product developments, industry news, and company strategies. Each issue features in-depth analysis of major CD-ROM developers and their activities. Quarterly supplements will list every commercially sold CD-ROM in existence.

Clients also receive a subscription to *CD-ROM Review* which covers all aspects of the CD-ROM industry. They also get a toll-free number which they can use to call the CIS staff at any time to discuss CD-ROM technology and issues.

Tools

The products discussed in this chapter and Chapter 5 cover one side of the CD-ROM story. They represent off-the-shelf, pre-packaged information. Another part of the story would see librarians and information providers mastering institution-specific data on CD-ROM. Several companies produce tools and provide services to assist in this endeavor.

Borland developed a set of tools for data search and retrieval for CD-ROM and other mass storage devices that need text retrieval capabilities. Going under the name "linguistic technology," these tools include a software engine, called the Finder, which can be adapted to several Borland WordBases (collections of terms for several vertical applications).

WordBases contain plural and inflected forms of words as well as several hyphenated terms and a 300,000-word thesaurus with more than 30,000 roots. Borland plans to create eleven language versions which will distinguish between American English and British English as well as between French and Canadian French.

CD Prep

Data Horizons, an optical scanning service bureau, launched a new data preparation service for CD-ROM publishers called CD Prep. It offers both text and image capture from a single source. Publishers of full-text databases traditionally send the text portion to an off-shore facility for keying and purchase image scanning equipment to convert the images.

Data Horizons uses the Palantir Compound Document Processor and customized software to scan both text and image in a single pass while maintaining the integrity of each. The company can scan, edit, and format up to 2,000 pages per day. This lets publishers take full advantage of the capabilities of both OCR and image scanning technology available from a single source.

CD Publisher

Meridian Data, Inc. produces CD Publisher, a large-capacity hard disk and tape subsystem that serves as an in-house CD-ROM premastering and simulation tool. It connects to an IBM XT or AT to permit creation of a fully tested, formatted, premaster tape ready for disc pressing. Meridian Data says that anybody who knows MS-DOS or PC-DOS and has some experience with database design, such as using a PC to create, manipulate, and store files, can prepare a CD-ROM premaster tape.

When not used for CD-ROM applications, the CD Publisher can serve as auxiliary memory for the PC. While its price (ranging from $28,000 for 300MB to $79,900 for 2400MB of memory) puts it beyond the means of most libraries, its existence demonstrates the importance and potential of CD-ROM.

To demonstrate the relative ease of mastering a CD-ROM disc, Philips Dupont Optical Company produced CD-ROM: The Conference Disc '87 (now out of print) at the 1987 Microsoft CD-ROM conference. This demonstration disc includes several CD-ROM retrieval packages accessing small- to medium-sized databases. It also includes some information gathered from the conference itself such as speeches, scanned images, OCR text, digitized pictures, and audio. Computer Access Corp. produced a disc of the first Microsoft conference entitled CD-ROM: The New Papyrus and Discovery Systems has a sampler disc to demonstrate the CD-ROM's capacity to integrate text, sound, graphics, and computer software.

CD Master and CD Network

Meridian Data introduced its CD Master and CD Network systems at the 1988 Microsoft Conference. CD Master is an encoding system that can master both CD audio and CD-ROM. CD Network and CD Server accommodate multiple users in a local area network environment. The unique difference between the two consists in CD Server's capability to combine and process incoming data from all sources including CD-ROM.

The number of products announced and in prototype indicate that 1988 will see further proliferation of CD-ROM databases. Two years ago, few information producers had optical products. Today, virtually every one has one or more discs on the market or under development—a sign that the medium has proven itself and gained acceptance.

CHAPTER 7
FUTURE PROJECTIONS

The earliest CD-ROM databases grew out of large public domain sources. These were soon followed by other large databases available in the commercial sector. More recently, publishers offered discs that contained a collection of databases on a single disc, thereby giving users a single source for searching several databases in the same subject area.

While the operator had to access each of these databases individually, the subscriber usually found that the collection provided more value than each one taken by itself. The next phase of multiple database CD-ROM products saw the integration of several knowledge bases on a single disc searched as a unit.

We are beginning to see products that exploit the technology in improved retrieval software such as windowing, graphics applications, saving of searches or strategies for transfer to magnetic disks or to online databases, and post-processing of search results by interfacing with external software packages like word processors and spreadsheets.

Librarians have also expressed the need for a better method of accessing CD-ROM discs. A short term solution to heavy patron demand could daisy-chain several drives together or use a jukebox device to hold multiple discs for use at a workstation.

While this solution may eliminate the need for changing discs, it will not do away with the problem of one user per workstation. Librarians need to provide multiple access points—including remote ones—to their collection of CD-ROM databases.

Local area networks will allow users to access any disc in the library through any connected workstation or PC. As the computer technology continues to increase in speed, more than one user will be able to access the same CD-ROM disc simultaneously. Remote access to such a system through the local telephone service will provide local and remote access to the databases.

Although patrons will not handle the CD-ROM discs and software, they will be able to search any database offered by the library. Such systems should become a reality in 1988 as several publishers have been testing systems and are redesigning the hardware and software necessary to meet the needs of libraries with expanding CD-ROM collections.[1]

Along with local area networking, we can expect to see multi-user, multi-tasking capabilities developed in the near to mid-term. In such an environment, librarians will administer the system by adding new databases, changing the menu of available files, and authorizing passwords for remote access.

Networking possibilities already exist; but, in addition to the issues related to maintaining high performance specifications, they present pricing/revenue and royalty questions which have not yet been resolved. This, along with slower response times, represents major reasons for discouraging their use at present.

Multi-Media CD-ROMs

We can also expect to see products with broader data formats than just text. Although a few prototype and sample CD-ROM discs exist with multi-media data, we can anticipate greater integration of various types of formats for more integrated approaches to information.

The use of hypertext/hypermedia to link ideas across the disc and across media present interesting challenges and opportunities. Such systems will combine artificial intelligence techniques with the large storage capacities of optical disks. A few prototypes have already appeared in demonstrations. Companies like the Del Mar Group, Inc. are developing others.

Such systems will also require integrated workstations (otherwise known as "scholarly workstations") to access information regardless of the medium: online, magnetic disk, videodisc, CD-ROM, WORM, or compact disc—interactive (CD-I) and regardless of the format: text, audio (analog or digital, voice grade, telephone grade, FM grade, or hi-fi), or graphics (still, stop-motion or full-motion video, computer-generated images, animation, CAD/CAM, etc.).

Integrated Workstations

Existing workstations provide a few of these options. Many CD-ROM drives have the capability of daisy-chaining several drives together to increase data access without having to change discs. Some devices have a combination of both CD-ROM and videodisc drives built in. Manufacturers are developing "omni" drives to permit the use of discs regardless of their size (3.5", 4.72", 5.25", 8", 12", or 14") or format (videodisc, WORM, CD-ROM, CD-I, or erasable).

Some products implementing some of these features, known as "combi" drives, have begun to appear on the market. These devices should eventually offer users the option of switching between CLV (constant linear velocity) and CAV (constant angular velocity) which permits freeze-frame capabilities.

We can also expect to see improvements in error detection and correction techniques which will permit greater data compression. On the other hand, we should also see disc capacity increase from the current 600- to 670-megabyte (MB) level to 750MB and more through the use of narrower tracks, focusing or media "tuning" (reducing the laser wavelength), or multi-level recording.

Multi-level recording presents several possibilities: polarizing the laser, "writing" at various depths of the disc surface, or recording at various frequencies in the color spectrum. This last technique maximizes disc real estate by using lasers tuned to different color combinations (frequencies) to record multiple data elements at the same address. This could increase disc capacities by a factor of 100.

Doubling Disc Capacity

The use of both sides of a disc for recording data would double its capacity. In addition, better searching algorithms would reduce seek time. Multiple heads (whether on the same side or on opposite sides of the disc—for double-sided systems) would decrease data access time. The young optical information industry is developing rapidly.

The future holds many promises and possibilities. The key to success for optical databases will lie in the packaging of appropriate data, improved access, better tools for using and managing information, the value added via cost benefits, and the identification of real market needs.

Notes

1. Pooley, Christopher. (1987). The CD-ROM Marketplace: A Producer's Perspective. *Wilson Library Bulletin.* 62:4, 24–26.

BIBLIOGRAPHY

An Introduction to Compact Disc-Interactive. (1987). Eindhoven, The Netherlands: New Media Information Center, Philips International B.V.

Artlip, P.M. (1987). How to Choose the Right Media: Optical, Magnetic, or Microfilm. *Journal of Information and Image Management* 18:9, 14–17.

Barney, Ron (1986). Betting on CD-ROM. *Electronic Publishing Business* 4:5, 12–13.

Barrett, R. (1982). Developments in Optical Disk Technology and the Implications for Information Storage and Retrieval. *Journal of Micrographics* 15:1, 22–26.

Befeler, Michael G. (1985). Laserdisc Systems from Reference Technology: Multiuser Technology for High-Use Environments. *Library Hi Tech* 3:2 (consecutive issue 10), 55–59.

Berg, Brian A. (1987). Critical Considerations for WORM Software Development. *Optical Information Systems.* 7:5, 329–333.

Billings, Sandra. (1986). Optical Storage Not an Option for National Archives, Study Concludes. *Video Computing.* Sept./Oct., 5.

Bowers, Richard A. (1987). *Optical Publishing Directory.* 2nd ed. Medford, NJ: Learned Information.

Brennan, Laura (1987). Microsoft Fulfills CD-ROM Pledge with Reference Disk. *PC Week* 4:8, 4.

Brewer, Brian. (1987). CD-ROM and CD-I. *CD-ROM Review.* 2:3, 18–25.

Buddine, Laura. (1987). *Brady Guide to CD-ROM.* New York: Prentice-Hall.

Campbell, Brian. (1987). Whither the White Knight: CD-ROM in Technical Services. *Database* 10:4, 22–40.

CD-ROM: Revolution Maker. (1986). COINT Reports: Vol. 6., No. 5. Morton Grove, IL: Info Digest.

CD-ROM vs. Hard Copy: Pricing. (1987). *Optical Information Systems Update/Library & Information Center Applications* 2:3, 15.

Cohen, Elaine, and Margo Young. (1986). Cost Comparison of Abstracts and Indexes on Paper, CD-ROM, and Online. *Optical Information Systems.* 6:6, 485–490.

Crane, Nancy and Tamara Durfee. (1987). Entering Uncharted Territory: Putting CD-ROM in Place. *Wilson Library Bulletin* 62:4, 28-30.

Criswell, L.B. (1983). Serials on Optical Disks: A Library of Congress Pilot Program. *Library Hi Tech.* 1:3, 17–21.

Davis, Susan. (1986). *CD-ROM: Technology and Applications.* White Plains, NY: Knowledge Industry.

DEMAND Printing in Library of Congress Cataloging Distribution Service (CDS). (1984). *Videodisc/Videotex.* 4:1, 22–25.

Desmarais, Norman. (1986). Laser Libraries. *Byte.* 11:5, 235–246.

———. (1987). Information Management on a Compact Silver Disc. *Optical Information Systems.* 7:3, 193–204.

———. (1987). Laserbases for Library Technical Services. *Optical Information Systems.* 7:1, 57–61.

———. (1987). The Status of CD-ROM Standards. *CD-ROM Librarian.* 2:4, 11–15.

———. (1988). Experiments Increase Optical Storage Densities. *Optical Information Systems* 8:1, 120–122.

Duchesne, Roddy, and Sabine S. Sonnemann. (1985). *Optical Disk Technology and the Library. Canadian Network Papers; No. 9.* National Library of Canada, Office for Network Development, Ottowa.

Freedman, Beth. (1986). Lotus Introduces CD-ROM System. *PC Week.* 3:39, 8.

Freese, Robert, Maarten DaHaan, and Albert Jamberdino (Eds.). (1986). *Optical Mass Data Storage II.* (SPIE vol. 695). Bellingham, WA: SPIE (The International Society for Optical Engineering).

Freund, Alfred L. (1985). A Regional Bibliographic Database on Videodisc. *Library Hi Tech* 3:2 (consecutive issue 10), 7–9.

Gale, J.C. (1984). Use of Optical Disks for Information Storage and Retrieval. *Information Technology and Libraries.* 3:4, 379–382.

———. (1985). The Information Workstation: A Confluence of Technologies Including the CD-ROM. *Information Technology and Libraries.* 4:2, 137–139.

———. (1987). Organizations Hash Out CD-ROM Standards. Compatibility Issues. *Computerworld* Aug. 24, 67-68.

Gibbins, Patrick. (1984). Electronic Publishing: The Future Convergence of Many Disciplines. *Journal of Information Science* 8:3, 123–129.

Giles, Peter. (1987). Optical Disk Applications: Now That We Have Them—What Are They Good For? *IMC Journal.* July–Aug., 22–23.

Goldstein, Charles M. (1984). Computer-Based Information Storage Technologies. *Annual Review of Information Science and Technology.* 19, 66–96.

Harris, Patricia. (1988). NISO CD-ROM Standards Update. *CD-ROM Librarian* 3:1, 8-9.

Helgerson, Linda W. (1985). CD-ROM Technology: A New Era for Information Storage and Retrieval. *Online* (Nov.), 17–28.

———. (1985). The Optical Disk as an Information Storage Tool. *Office Administration and Automation* (April), 47–49, 70-72.

———. (1985). Optical Technology: Impact on information transfer. *Bowker Annual of Library and Book Trade Information.* New York, London: R.R. Bowker Co., pp. 91–102.

———. (1986). CD-ROM: A Revolution in the Making. *Library Hi-Tech.* 4:1, 23–27

——— (Ed.). (1987). *CD-ROM Sourcebook.* Falls Church, VA: DDRI.

———. (1987). Keep in Touch. *Computer Systems News.* 309, S36–39.

——— and Martin Ennis. (1987). *CD-ROM Sourcedisc.* (1987). Falls Church, VA: Diversified Data Resources, Inc.

Hendley, A.M. (1985). *Videodiscs, Compact Discs, and Digital Optical Disks: An Introduction to the Technologies and the Systems and Their Potential for Information Storage, Retrieval and Dissemination.*—CIMTECH Publication; 23. CIMTECH, The National Center for Information Media Technology, Hatfield, Herts, England.

Hendley, Tony. (1987). *CD-ROM and Optical Publishing Systems.* Westport, CT: Meckler Publishing Corp.; Hatfield, England: Cimtech.

Hensel, M. and R. Nelson. (1984). CD-ROM: Dramatic Key to Information Dissemination and Use. *Electronic Library* 2:4, 257–259.

Herther, Nancy K. (1985). CD-ROM Technology: A New Era For Information Storage and Retrieval. *Online* 9:6, 17–28.

———. (1986). Access Software for Optical/Laser Information Packages. *Database.* 9:4, 93–97.

———. (1987). Between a Rock and a Hard Place: Preservation and Optical Media. *Database.* 10:12, 122–124.

———. (1987). CD-ROM and Information Dissemination: An Update. *Online* 10:2, 56–64.

———. (1987). A Planning Model for Optical Product Evaluation. *Online* 10:5, 128–130.

Hessler, David W. (1984). Interactive Optical Disc Systems. *Library Hi Tech* 2:4 (consecutive issue 8), 25–31.

Hooton, William L. (1985). The Optical Digital Image Storage

System (ODISS) at the National Archives and Records Administration, in *1985 Videodisc, Optical Disk, and CD-ROM Conference & Exposition,* pp. 90–95. Westport, CT: Meckler Publishing.

———. (1986). An Update on the Optical Digital Image Storage System (ODISS) at the National Archives, in Judith Paris Roth (Comp.), *Optical Information Systems '86,* pp. 153–157. Westport, CT: Meckler Publishing Corp.

Isailovic, Jordan. (1985). *Videodisc and Optical Memory Systems.* Englewood Cliffs, NJ: Prentice-Hall.

———. (1987). *Videodisc Systems: Theory and Applications.* Englewood Cliffs, NJ: Prentice-Hall.

Isbouts, Jean-Pierre. (1987). A User-Friendly Guide for Videodisc Producers. *Videodisc Monitor.* June 16–19.

Janus, Susan. (1987). IBM 5.25-inch WORM Disk Drive Could Turn the Direction of Standard. *PC Week* 4:25, 107.

Krayeski, Felix and Tamara Swora. (1985). Image Processing and Optical Disk Technology at the Library of Congress and the Congressional Research Service. In *1985 Videodisc, Optical Disk, and CD-ROM Conference & Exposition Conference Proceedings,* pp. 111–118. Westport, CT: Meckler Publishing.

Lambert, Steve and Suzanne Ropiequet (Eds.). (1986). *CD ROM: The New Papyrus: The Current and Future State of the Art.* Redmond, WA: Microsoft Press.

Laser Bases: Laserdisc and CD-ROM Databases for Local and Inhouse Use. (1985). (Library Hi Tech Special Studies Series, 2). Ann Arbor, MI: Pierian Press.

The Library of Congress: Optical Disk Pilot Program. (1983). *Records Management Quarterly* 17, 50–51.

Liebaers, Herman, Warren J. Hass, and Wim Biervliet (Eds.). (1985). *New Information Technologies and Libraries.* Dordrecht, The Netherlands: D. Reidel, 1985.

Luhn, Robert, David Bunnell, and Harry Miller. (1987). PC World CD-ROM Forum. *PC World.* 5:4, 220–230.

Market for Optical-Disk Storage Systems Shows Enormous Promise. (1987). *Computer Reseller News.* 202, 79-80.

Marmion, Dan. (1987). Installing CD-ROM Systems: How Do We Do It? *CD-ROM Librarian* 2:6, 16-20.

Mason, Robert M. (1985). Laser Disks for Micros. *Library Journal* (Feb. 19), 124-125.

McManus, Reed. (1986). CD-ROM: The Little Leviathan. *PC World* 4, 273-280.

McQueen, Judy and Richard W. Boss. (1986). *Videodisc and Optical Disk Technologies and Their Applications in Libraries: 1986 Update.* Chicago: American Library Association.

Miller, David. (1987). Special Report: Publishers, Libraries & CD-ROM: Implications of Digiral Optical Printing. Portland, OR: DCM Associates; Chicago: American Library Association.

Miller, David C. (1987). Evaluating CD-ROMs: To Buy or What to Buy? *Database* 10:3, 36-42.

Miller, Tim. (1987). "Early User Reaction to CD-ROM and Videodisc-Based Optical Information Products in the Library Market. *Optical Information Systems* 7:3, 205-209.

Murphy, Brower. (1985). Libraries and CD-ROM: A Special Report. *Small Computers in Libraries* 5 (April), 7-10.

Myers, Patti. (1987). *Publishing with CD-ROM: A Guide to Compact Disc Optical Storage Technologies for Providers of Publishing Services.* Westport, CT: Meckler Corp.

Nelson, Nancy. (1987). The CD-ROM Industry: A Library Market Overview. *Wilson Library Bulletin* 62:4, 19-20.

———— (comp.). (1987). *CD-ROMs in Print 1987.* Westport, CT and London: Meckler.

————. (1987). *Library Applications of Optical Disk and CD-ROM Technology. Essential Guide to the Library IBM-PC,* vol. 8. Westport, CT: Meckler Corp.

Newhard, Robert. (1987). Converting Information into Knowledge: The Promise of CD-ROM. *Wilson Library Bulletin* 62:4, 36-38.

NISO Standards Update. (1987). *CD-ROM Librarian.* 2:4, 15-16.

Nofel, P.J. (1985). News & Trends: Desktop Databases: Gigabytes of CD-ROM. *Modern Office Technology* 30:4, 46-47.

Optical and Magnetic Disk Media—Report—International Resources Development, Inc.: #620. Norwalk, CT: International Resources Development.

Pemberton, Jeff. (1986). Shooting Ourselves in the Foot...And Other Consequences of Laserdisks. *Online.* 9:3, 9-11.

Pezzanite, Frank A. (1985). The LC MARC Database on Video Laserdisc: The MINI MARC System. *Library Hi Tech* 3:1 (consecutive issue 9), 57-60.

Pooley, Christopher. (1987). The CD-ROM Marketplace: A Producer's Perspective. *Wilson Library Bulletin* 62:4, 24-26.

Porter, M. (1985). Compact Discs Pack in Data. *High Technology* 5:1, 64, 66, 68.

Preservation of Historical Records—The National Archives & Records Administration Study of Preservation Media. Washington, DC: National Academy of Sciences.

Price, Joseph. (1984). The Optical Disk Pilot Program at the Library of Congress. *Videodisc and Optical Disk.* 4:6, 424-432.

Putting into Perspective the Mind-Boggling Storage Power of CD-ROMs (1985). *InfoWorld* Sept. 23, 29.

Raimondi, Donna. (1986). Security Pacific Banks on Optical Disk Systems. *Computerworld* 20:45, 14.

Ropiequet, Suzanne. (1986). *Optical Publishing.* CD-ROM Series; 2. Redmond, WA: Microsoft Press.

———, John Einberger and Bill Zoellick (Eds.). (1987). *CD-ROM: Optical Publishing* (vol. II). Redmond, WA: Microsoft Publishing.

Rosenthal, Steve. (1986). Optical Data Disks May Up RAM Space But Sacrifice Speed. *PC Week* 3:9, 124–125.

Roth, Judith Paris (Ed.). (1986). *Essential Guide to CD-ROM* (1986). Westport, CT: Meckler Publishing Company.

Rothchild, Edward. (1983). Optical-Memory Media: How Optical Disks Work, Who Makes Them, and How Much Data They Can Hold. *Byte* 8, 86–106.

———. (1984). Optical Memory: Data Storage by Laser. *Byte* 9 (Oct.), 215–224.

Saffady, William. (1985). *Optical Disks 1985: A State of the Art Review.* Westport, CT: Meckler Publishing.

———. (1985). *Optical Disks for Data and Documents Storage.* Westport, CT: Meckler Publishing.

———. (1987). *Optical Storage Technology 1987: A State of the Art Review.* Westport, CT: Meckler Corp.

Schaub, John A. (1985). CD-ROM For Public Access Catalogs. *Library Hi Tech.* consecutive issue 11, 7–13.

Schwerin, Julie B. (1984). The Reality of Information Storage, Retrieval and Display Using Videodiscs. *Videodisc and Optical Disk* 4:2, 113–121.

———. (1985). Optical Systems for Information Delivery and Storage. *Electronic Publishing Review* 5:3, 193–198.

———. (1986). *CD-ROM Standards: The Book.* Oxford, England: Learned Information; Pittsfield, VT: InfoTech.

Seymour, Jim. (1986). Awaiting the CD-ROM Boom. *PC.* 5:10, 87–88.

Sinnett, Dennis and Sheila Edwards. (1984). Authoring Systems: The Key to Widespread Use of Interactive Videodisc Technology. *Library Hi Tech* 2:4 (consecutive issue 8), 39–50.

Spiter, Gerald A. (1987). *The Disconnection: Interactive Video and Optical Disc Media.* White Plains: Knowledge Industry Publications, Inc.

Stewart, Linda. (1987). Picking CD-ROMs for Public Use. *American Libraries.* 18:9, 738–740.

Sustar, Lee. (1986). 3M Forges Optical Disk Alliances. *MIS Week* 7:39, 12.

Tenopir, Carol. (1987). Costs and Benefits of CD-ROM. *Library Journal.* 112:14, 156–157.

Tri-Star Publishing Releases its Trademark Research System. (1987). *CD Data Report* 3:7, 6–7.

Videodisc and Optical Disk Technologies and Their Applications in Libraries: A Report to the Council on Library Resources. (1985). Washington, DC: Information Systems Consultants.

Vizachero, Rick. (1986). Optical Storage Gets Agencies' Attention. *Government Computer News.* 12-5.

Weissman, Steven B. (1987). Coping with Change. *Computer Systems News.* 309, S40–41.

Welch, Randy. (1986). A New Stab at Data Storage. *Venture* Feb., 68.

INDEX

1929-1986 Business Indicators CD-ROM 111
1987 Registry of Mass Spectral Data 128

ABI/INFORM 87, 103
ABI/Inform Ondisc 99
Abridged Index Medicus Brandon/Hill journal lists 117
Academic American Encyclopedia 83
Academic Index 90
Access Softek 86
Access software 5
Access time 30, 44
Accura Parts Catalog 114
Address Verification System Plus (AVS+) 114
ADONIS CD-ROM Biomedical Collection 118
ADONIS database 119
Advanced searchers 76, 95
AGRICOLA 94, 97
Agriculture Materials in Libraries (AgMIL) 97
AIRS Inc. 88
ALANET 99
ALDE Publishing 114, 122, 123, 136
Alternative sources 2
Amdek 29, 31
American Heritage Dictionary 85
American Library Association 69
American Psychological Association 93
Amiga. *See* Commodore Amiga
Any-Book 15, 81, 82
AppleCD-SC 31
Apple Computer, Inc. 31, 39, 126
Apple Macintosh. *See* Macintosh
Apple IIe 86
Application level standardization 19, 20
Applied Science & Technology Index 95
Aquatic Sciences & Fisheries Abstracts (ASFA) 118
Aries Systems Corporation 117
Art Index 95
Artificial intelligence 27, 82, 108, 142
Atlanta Constitution 87, 88, 99
Atlanta Journal 87, 99

155

Authorities Collection 73
Authority control features 5
Autocad 130
Autodesk Inc. 130
AutoGraphics Inc. 77
AV Online 93

Baker & Taylor 80, 82
Bartlett's Familiar Quotations 85
BBC Domesday Project 135
Bell & Howell 114
BIBL file 101
Bible Library on CD-ROM 88
BiblioFile 69, 70, 75
BiblioFile Catalog Production System 82
Bibliographic instruction sessions 51
Bibliographic Processing Network 71
BiblioMed 118
Bio-ROM 119
Biography Index 95
BioLibe 120
Biological & Agricultural Index 95
Biomedical Document Delivery Service (BDDS) 119
BIOREP 119
Black Fiction to 1920 125
Blackwell 80
Blackwell Scientific Publications Ltd. 119
Blue Bear Group Inc. 78
Blue Sail Software Inc. 136
BlueFish 105
Book Review Digest 95
Books in Print 79
Books in Print Plus 48, 79, 81, 96
Books in Print with Reviews Plus 80
Books Out of Print Plus 80
Bookshelf, *See* Microsoft Bookshelf
Boolean logic 78-80, 83, 96, 98, 127
Boolean operators 6, 86, 95
Boolean search 44, 53, 54, 74-77, 87, 88, 99
Borland 139
Bowker Electronic Publishing 83
Bowker 79-81, 96
Brandon/Hill journal lists 117

British Books in Print 74, 81
British Library 73, 74, 129
British Post Office 115
Brodart 74, 80
Brodart Automation 78
BRS Information Technologies 87, 116, 117
BRS/Colleague Disc 116
Buchhandler Vereinigung GmbH 81
Budgeting 16, 50, 52, 72
Building Sciences Information 129
Bulletin board 75, 136
Bureau of the Census. *See* U.S. Bureau of the Census
Business Base 115
Business Information Sources 85
Business Periodicals Index 95
Business Research Corp. 103
Business Software Database 94
Butterworth Scientific Ltd. 119

CaCD (Cancer Abstracts) 93
Caddy 29
California Manufacturers' Directory 109
Cambridge Scientific Abstracts 118, 128
Canada Centre for Remote Sensing (CCRS) 129
Canadian Centre for Occupational Health and Safety 120
Canadian Federal Department of Energy Mines and Regulation 129
CANADIANA 120
CARIN (Car Information and Navigation) 132
Carrollton Press 70
Cascading 92
CAT CD450 72-73
Cataloging Distribution Service 71-72
CCINFO CD-ROM line 120
CD Master 140
CD Network 140
CD Prep 139
CD Publisher 140
CD-ROM Continuous Information Service 138
CD-ROM drive 25, 27-38, 42, 46, 86, 143
CD-ROM Extensions 21-23, 26, 30, 31, 39, 41-43
CD-ROM Lab Report 138
CD-ROM Librarian 5
CD-ROM Review 5, 138, 139

158 The Librarian's CD-ROM Handbook

CD-ROM Source Disc 86
CD-ROM vs. online 50
CD-ROM: The Conference Disc '87 140
CD-ROM: The New Papyrus (disc) 140
CD-Yellow Pages 110
CD/2000 77, 78
CD/Banking 105, 107
CD/Biotech 118
CD/Corporate 103-106
CD/International 105-107
CD/Newsline 105
CD/Private+ 105
CDA Investment Technologies Inc. 103
CDMARC Names 72
CDMARC Subjects 72
Cellular phone 66
Census Bureau. *See* U.S. Bureau of the Census
Census of Agriculture 111
Center for International Financial Analysis and Research 106
Chadwyck-Healey Inc. 112
Charging patrons 17, 64
ChemBank 94
Cheminfo 120
Chicago Manual of Style 85
Chicken-and-egg syndrome 60
CHI-Writer 89
CHRIS (Chemical Hazard Response Information System) 94
Christian Science Monitor 87, 99
Chronological segmentation 2
Chrysler 133
Chrysler Parts Catalog 114
Churchill Livingstone 119
CineScan 137
CISDOC 94
CL-Medline 118
CLASIX system 129
CLSI Inc. 117
Code of Federal Regulations. See U.S. Code of Federal Regulations
Code of the Commonwealth of Virginia 121
Colleague search software 117
Collection development policies 3, 49
College Blue Book 126
"Combi" drives 143
Command stacking 6

Commercial Banks Database 107
Commodore Amiga 26
Communist Manifesto 123
Compact Cambridge 118
Compact Disclosure 103
Compact Discoveries 110
Compact Solution 84
Comprehensive Dissertation Index 87
Compu-Info 94
Compustat 107
Computer Access Corporation 105, 140
Computerized Clinical Information System (CCIS) 116
Comsell 110
Congressional Record 100
Conquest Consumer Information System 108
Constant angular velocity 143
Constant linear velocity 143
Content and scope of the laserbase 52, 56, 65
Controller card 8, 26, 28, 42
Convenience 3, 47, 49, 55
Conversion costs 65
Copyright issues 60, 64, 85, 100
Cornell University 125
Corporate and Industry Research Reports (CIRR) 94
Corporate Information Database 103
Corporate Technology Information Services (CTIS) 104
Cost 14-18, 45, 50, 64, 65, 72, 133, 134
Cost decreases 52
Cost effectiveness 18, 47, 57, 62
COSTAT2 tape 111
County Statistics 111
CrossLink 130
Cumulative Book Index 95
Current Research Information System 97
Customer support 7

Daily Oklahoman 136
Daily Stock Price History 107
Daisy-chain 56, 70, 98, 141, 143
Dante project 125
Dartmouth College 125
Data access time 13, 143
Data Archive on Adolescent Pregnancy 86
Data Base Products Inc. 134

Data compression 143
Data conversion 62
Data Courier 103
Data error detection. *See* Error detection and correction techniques
Data Horizons 139
Data permanence 59, 62-63
Data reliability 63
Data transfer rate 30
Datatek 136
DataTimes 136
Datext 103-107
DECUS 135
Del Mar Group 75, 82, 108, 142
DeLorme Global Mapper 131
DeLorme Mapping Systems 131-132
Denon 31, 38
Derwent Publications 115, 119
Desktop-publishing systems 41
Device driver 21-23, 41, 43, 48
Diacritics 74
DIALOG 87
DIALOG Information Services 91
Dialog OnDisc line 91, 92, 117
Digital Decus Group 135
Digital Diagnostics 118
Digital Equipment Corp. 32
Digital Information Group 14
Directory of Leading Private Companies 105
Directory of Library & Information Professionals 86
Disc ownership 49, 64
Disc Print Pilot Project 100
DISCAT 70
Disclosure II 103, 107
Disclosure Information Group 90, 91, 103
Disclosure/Spectrum Stock Ownership Database 103
DISCON 70
Discovery Systems 140
Dissertation Abstracts International 87
Dissertation Abstracts Ondisc 87
Diversified Data Resources Inc 86
Documentation 7, 44, 54, 105, 113, 128
Documentation Archetype Systems 124
DOCUSYSTEM, software and hardware for 84
Donnelly Marketing Information Services 108

DOS patches 21, 41
DoveSystem 137
Dow Jones & Co. 105
Dragnet 86
Drugdex 116
Dun & Bradstreet 108
Duplication 49

EBSCO Serials Directory 48
Editions Quebec/Amerique Inc. 85
Education Index 95
Education Materials in Libraries (EMIL) 97
EGA 27
Electronic Data Systems 135
The Electronic Encyclopedia 83
Electronic mail 78, 85, 99
Electronic order 80, 82
Electronic Publishing Abstracts 85
Ellis Enterprises Inc. 88
Elsevier Science Publishers 93
EMBASE (Excerpta Medica) 3, 93, 119
Emergindex/Diagnostics and Therapeutics 116
ENFLEX INFO 124
Engineering Information Systems 129
Environmental Resources Management (ERM) 124
Erasable discs 59
ERIC 2, 91-92, 98
Error detection and correction techniques 64, 143
Essay and General Literature Index 95
Eurolex 121
European Computer Manufacturers Association 19
European Molecular Biology Laboratory 118
European Radio Data System 133
Excerpta Medica (Netherlands) 119
Experienced users 53, 75, 77, 79
Expert systems 27
Exporting information 11

Facts on File Inc. 85
Facts on File News Digest 86
The Facts on File Visual Dictionary 85
False drops 5
Fast Past 126
The Faxon Company 83, 117, 119

FDIC 107
FEB on CD-ROM (FABS Electronic Bible) 89
Federal Acquisition/Procurement Disc (Title 41/48) 123
Federal Register 124
Federal Reserve Board 107
File structures 4
Finder 139
First National Item Bank and Test Development System 126
Fleet Management System Software 132
Focusing 143
Foundation for Advanced Biblical Studies 88
FRB on CD-ROM (FABS Reference Bible) 89
Freeze-frame capabilities 143
Friends of the Library 16
Frustration 3, 51, 56-57

Gaylord Bros. 71, 77
Genbank 118
General Research Corporation 69, 70, 76
General Science Index 95
Genetic Sequences Databank 118
GEOdisc 130
Geographic Data Technology Inc. 133
Georgia state disc 131
Geovision Inc. 130
Global Positioning Satellite (GPS) 134
GM Parts Catalog 114
Good Housekeeping 2
Government Documents Catalog Subscription (GDCS) 77
Government Printing Office 69, 71
Government Printing Office Catalog 77
Government Publications Index 90
GPO LASERFILE 71
GPO Monthly Catalog/Index to U.S. Government Periodicals 95
Grolier 83

H.W. Wilson. *See* Wilson
Halo (Media Cybernetics) 130
Hardware interface 8, 21
Hardware-software interface 8
Harvard University Press 125
Hatfield Polytechnic Institute 73
Hearst Metrotone News 137
Help messages 7

Hercules card 27
High Sierra Group 19-20, 22
High Sierra/NISO standard 30, 41, 43
Highlighted Data 85, 132
Hitachi 32, 38, 79, 132
Hitachi driver 41
Hitachi drives 29, 31, 38
Home Base 115
Honda Parts Catalog 114
Houghton Mifflin Spelling Verifier and Corrector 85
HSELINE 93
Humanities Index 95
Hydrodata 129
Hypermedia 142
Hypertext 10, 66, 127, 142

I.S. Group 120
IBM PC/XT/AT 26, 39, 136, 138
IBM PS/2 26, 138
Ibycus Systems 125
Icons 44, 84
Identidex/Tablet and Capsule Identification 116
IDG Communications 138
IDG Report on CD-ROM 138
IMPACT 77
Inacom International 129
Index to Legal Periodicals 95
Index to Periodical Literature 89
Indexing 3, 4, 74
Info Globe 136
Infomark 110
Infomark Laser PC System 109
Information Access Company 90, 121
Information Design Incorporated (IDI) 114
Information Handling Services 130
Information hierarchies 9-10
Information on Demand Inc. 119
Infoserv 119
InfoTrac 2, 90, 121
InfoTrac Reference Center 91
InfoTrac II 90
Ingram Book Company 80-82
Innovative Technology 130
Inserm France 119

Institute for Scientific Information (ISI) 96, 127
Intechnica Learning Systems Inc. 126
Integrated Logistics Service 113
Integrated workstations 142, 143
Intel 80286 and 80386 chips 26
The Intelligent Catalog 74-75
Interactive videodisc 54
Interage Research Inc. 126
Interfaces 8, 11, 38, 42, 46, 65
Interface card 27. *See also* Controller card
Interleaving 64
Interlibrary loan 3, 51, 78, 99
Internal Revenue Code 122
Internal Revenue Service 121
International Association for Scientific Computing 118
International Centre for Diffraction Data 128-129
International Computaprint Corp. 79, 115
International Dictionary of Medicine and Biology 128
International Electronic Publishing Research Centre 85
International Encyclopaedia of Education 84
International Occupational Safety and Health Information Centre 94
International Serials Database Update 80
International Standards Organization 19
International Thomson 70
Inventory Locator Service Inc. 113
Inverted indexing 4
Investext 103
Iowa Locater 78
Iowa State Library 78
Irregular Serials and Annuals 80
Izvestia 123

Japan Radio Co. 134
John Wiley & Sons 84, 119, 128
Johns Hopkins 118
Jukebox 21, 57, 65, 100, 141
JVC 34

KAware software 109
Keyword 9, 83, 87, 100, 118, 128
Keyword searching 10, 86
Kirk-Othmer Encyclopedia of Chemical Technology 128
Knowledge Access International 86, 109
Knowledge Retrieval System 84

Kwikee INHOUSE Graphic Services disc 136

LANDSAT 130, 131, 134
LaserCat 77
LaserData 108, 138
Laserdek 31
LaserGuide 76
LaserQuest 70
LaserSearch 82
Lasertrak Corporation 134
Lasertrak Pathfinder 134
LaserView turnkey system 138
Latency time 4, 30
LAWMARC 70, 120
LegalTrac 121
LePac 74
LePac: Interlibrary Loan Option 78
Librarian's Inquiry Terminal 82
The Library Corporation 15, 69, 74, 81, 82, 135
Library Literature 95
Library of Congress 69, 70, 83, 100
Library of Congress's Cataloging Distribution Service. *See* Cataloging Distribution Service
Library Systems & Services Inc. 71, 77
License agreements 3, 45, 49
Life Sciences Collection 118
Limit use 57
LinguaTech Bilingual Dictionary 126
LISA (Library & Information Science Abstracts) 93
Local area network 39, 40, 47, 69, 140, 141, 142. *See also* Networks
LoDown 38
Loeb classics 125
Logical standard 19-20
Lotus 1-2-3 104, 107, 112
Lotus Development Corporation 105, 107
LS/2000 78
Lucasfilm Ltd. 127
Lyndon B. Johnson Space Center 137

Macintosh 26, 37, 80, 117, 136
Magazine Index 90, 91, 101
Magneto-optic drives 59
Maintenance 42, 46, 48, 51, 62

The Map Cabinet 132
MARC 69-71, 76, 82, 98, 131
MARC-S Serials file 83
MARC tags 74, 75
MARCIVE Inc. 75-76
The Market File 104
Marquis Who's Who 104
MARVLS 70
Master Search 112-113
Material Safety Data System 130
Mayo Clinic 118
McGraw Hill Book Company 84, 127
The McGraw Hill Concise Encyclopedia of Science
 and Technology 84
McGraw Hill Dictionary of Scientific and Technical Terms 84
Mead Data Central 122
Medata-Rom 119
Media "tuning" 143
Medical Economics Company 120
MEDLARS 116
MEDLINE 92, 116-119
MEDLINE Knowledge Finder 117
MEDLINE on a SilverPlatter 93
Megazines series 118
Memory Requirements 27
Menu (software) 126
Mercury spacecraft 137
Meridian Data Inc. 22, 140
Merriam Webster Ninth New Collegiate Dictionary 85
The Michie Company 121
Microchannel bus architecture 26
Microcomputer Index 109
MicroLinx 83
Micromedex Inc. 116
MicroReviews 109
Microscan 107
Microsoft Bookshelf 29, 31, 38, 85, 115
Microsoft CD-ROM Conference 31, 140
Microsoft Corp. 21, 22, 26, 30, 85, 86
Microsoft "Windows" 86, 130
Microsoft's CD-ROM Extensions. *See* CD-ROM Extensions
MicroTrends Inc. 120, 126
MINI MARC 71
Mitsubishi Electric Corp. 134

MLA International Bibliography 95
Monitors 27
Mosby Company 119
Multi-Ad Services Inc. 136
Multi-file searching 56
Multi-level recording 143
Multi-Media CD-ROMs 63, 142
Multi-purpose products 48
Multi-user systems 13, 56, 65, 84, 140
Multi-user multi-tasking capabilities 40, 142
MultiMate 104
Multiple access points 141
Multiple heads 143
Munksgaard International Publications 119

N.V. Philips 133
Name authority records 72
Names In the News 99
NASA's Jet Propulsion Laboratory 125
National Agricultural Library 94, 97
National Archives and Records Administration 62-63
National Biomedical Research Foundation 118
National Cancer Institute 93
National Decision Systems 109
National Geographic Society 126
National Information Center for Educational Media (NICEM) 71, 93
National Information Standards Organization 6, 19, 20, 22
National Institute for Occupational Safety and Health 93-94, 120
National Institute of Builders 129
National Library of Canada 70
National Library of Medicine 92, 93, 116
National Oceanic and Atmospheric Administration 134
National Postal Service Directory 114
National Safety Data Corp. 129
National Standards Association 124
National Telephone Directory 85
Natural language 3, 74
Nature Plus 126
Navstar Global Positioning System 133
Neighboring 95
Nesting 6
Networking 126
Networks 25
New York Times 87, 90, 99

Newspaper Abstracts 87
Newspaper Abstracts Ondisc 99
NewsBank 99, 100
NewsBank Electronic Index 99
NewScan 137
NICEM: National Information Center for Educational Media 71, 93
NIOSHTIC 93, 120
NISO. *See* National Information Standards Organization
Novice user 6, 11, 53, 79, 91, 96, 117
NTIS 92
NTIS on a SilverPlatter 93
NTIS Science and Technology Materials in Libraries 98

O&D Plus 134
OCLC 69, 72, 73, 77-80, 97
OHMTADS Oil and Hazardous Materials—Technical Assistance Data 94
Older Books and Most-used Nonbook Cataloging Collection 72
"Omni" drives 143
Oncodisc 120
One Source 107
Online access 11
Online Computer Systems 26, 71, 77, 79, 81, 96, 121
Online news 105
Online search services 48, 55, 121
Online searching 50, 92
Online support 45
Online Union Catalog 72, 97
Online Union Catalog Resource Sharing component 99
Onsite Plus 114
OPTEXT Online Demo 123
Optical Digital Image Storage System Project (ODISS) 63
Optical Information Systems 5
Origin and Destination (O&D) Survey 135
OS/2 26-27
OSH-ROM 93
Oxford English Dictionary 83
Oxford University Press 84

PAIS on CD-ROM 96
Palantir Compound Document Processor 139
Panasonic 34, 38
Parametrix 129
Parts Master 124

Pascal 119
Pass-through billing 17
Patron assistance 48, 54-55
PC Laser Library 135
PCI Inc. 129
PC-SIG, Inc. 126, 135
PC-SIG Library 135
PC/MARC system 71
PDR Direct Access 120
Pergamon 85, 115
Pergamon Infoline 84
Periodic evaluation 57
Peripheral devices 28, 39
Personal Mapping System 132
Philips 19, 28, 29, 38, 61
Philips drives 32, 38, 52
Philips Dupont Optical Company 140
Philips/LMSI Laser Magnetic Storage International 32, 35
PHINet tax resource library 121
Physical standards 19
Poisindex 116
Pollution/Ecology/Toxicology 128
Poole's Index 89
Portable CD-ROM units 66
Post-processing 11-12, 44
Postcode Address File 115
Powder Diffraction File 129
Power user 53
Pravda 123
Predicasts 104
Prentice-Hall 121
Pricing 64, 142
Promt (database) 104
Proprietary computer 134
Proprietary device drivers 41
Proprietary interface cards 39
Proprietary software 20-22, 30, 106, 111, 112, 122, 130
Protein Identification Resource 118
Proximity operators 11, 88, 99
PS/2. *See* IBM PS/2
PsycINFO 92
PsycLit 2 92
Public Affairs Information Service Inc. 96
Public Health Code 122

Publicity 48

Quadram Corp. 110
QuadVision 110
Quality control 5
Quantum Access Inc. 122
Questel software 119, 129

R.R. Bowker. *See* Bowker
Radio Shack 29
RAINBOW " The Connection" series 115
Random House Dictionary 85
Reader's Advisory Assistance 75
Reader's Guide to Periodical Literature 2, 95
Real Estate Data Inc. 110
Real Estate Data: Washington DC Metro Area 110
Recent Books Cataloging Collection 72-73
Reed Publishing U.S.A. 79
Reference DataPlate 85
Reference policies 50
Reference Technology Inc. 36, 41, 84, 85, 108, 115, 121, 126, 129, 135,
Registry of Toxic Effects of Chemical Substances 94, 120
Regulatory Information on Pesticide Products 120
Relevancy and Scope of Search 2
Religious and Theological Abstracts 88
REMARC 70
Remote access 141-142
Research Publications 86
Resors database 129
Response time 13, 21, 55-56
Retailer's Assistant 108-109
Retrieval software 19, 77, 80, 141. *See also* Search and retrieval software
Review of the Arts 99
Reviewing media 5
REX on CD-ROM 88
Reynolds & Reynolds 114
Roget's Thesaurus 85
Royalty questions 142
RTECS 94

Sansyusa Publishing Company 85
Sanyo 36

Index   171

Scholarly Personal Computer   125
Scholarly workstations   142
Science and Technical Reference Set   127
Science and Technology Series   98
Science Citation Index (SCI)   127
Science Helper K-8   126
Scientific and Technical Reference Set   84
Scope of the database   1-2, 56, 65
SCORPIO commands   100
ScreenSheet   106
SCSI   21, 39-40
Seamless interface   3, 117
Search and retrieval software   3, 44, 47, 65, 86, 105, 121, 128
Search CD450   97-98, 117
SEARCHER   111
Searching algorithms   143
Sears   29
Secondary users   64
Securities and Exchange Commission (SEC)   103
Security   29, 48, 51-52
"See" references   5, 95, 96, 99
Seek rates   59
Seek time   30, 143
Selectory   109
The Serials Directory/EBSCO CD-ROM   82
Service contract   43
SFM Media Corporation   137
Shakespeare project   125
Sherman Grindberg Library   137
Sheshunoff & Co.   107
Shugart Associates Standard Interface   39
SilverPlatter Information Services   91-93, 115, 120
Single-user systems   64-65
Slater Hall Information Products   111-112
Small Computer Systems Interface. *See* SCSI
Social Sciences Index   95
Social Security Database   122
Sociofile   93
Sociological Abstracts   93
Sociometrics Corporation   86
Software interface   81
Software obsolescence   62
Software quality   4
Sony   19, 29, 36, 38, 59, 61, 79

Space Shuttle Columbia 137
Space-Time Research 112
Spectrum 200 77
Speech recognition 85
Speech synthesis unit 133
Springer-Verlag GmbH 119
Standard and Poor's 107
Standardization 6, 18-23, 39, 60
Stanford University 125
State Education Encyclopedia 122
Subject authority record 72
Supermap 112
Survey of Current Business 111
Syntax errors 6
System configurations 48
System Development Corporation 63
System evaluation 48

Tacoma Public Library 75
Tandy Corp. 29
TASS 123
Tax Analysts 115, 121
Tax Court Opinions 115
Tax Notes Today 115, 121
Tech-Doc/Digital Data laserbase 129
Technical Logistics Reference Network 130
Teleflora 136
Telesystemes 119
Tescor Inc. 126
Tetragon 115
Texas Attorney General Documents 122
Thesaurus Linguae Graecae 125
TMS 122, 131
TMS search software 122
Toronto Globe and Mail 136
Toshiba 37
Tradenames 120
Tri Star Publishing 83, 90, 112-113, 125
Trident submarine 124-125
Truncation 6, 70, 77, 80, 88, 95, 96, 99, 127
Tutorials 7, 44, 54, 88, 99, 126

U.S. Bureau of the Census 111, 130-131
U.S. Bureau of the Census Census Test Disc 112

U.S. Code of Federal Regulations 122-123
U.S. Department of Agriculture 97
U.S. Department of Commerce 111
U.S. Department of Customs 135
U.S. Department of Defense 114
U.S. Department of Transportation 94, 134
U.S. Environmental Protection Agency 94
U.S. Geological Service Daily Values 129
U.S. Geological Survey 131
U.S. Government Printing Office. *See* Government Printing Office
U.S. National Institute for Occupational Safety and Health 120
U.S. Patent and Trademark Office 112
U.S. Post Office 123
U.S. WEST Knowledge Engineering 126, 129
U.S. Zip Code Directory 85
UKMARC 74
Ulrich's International Periodicals Directory 79, 80
Ulrich's Plus 48, 79-80, 82
University College London 73
University Microfilms International 87, 99, 104, 118
University of Birmingham 73
University of California, Irvine 125
University of Loughborough 73
User interface 8-13, 21, 43, 60, 78, 99
User-friendliness 5
Users 52-54, 55-57, 60
USSR Source 21, 123
UTLAS 70, 120

Value Line 107
Versa Text 126
Verzeichnis Lieferbarer Bucher 81
VGA graphics adapter 27
Videodisc 70
The Virginia Disc: An Evaluation of Locally Produced CD-ROM Products 131
Virginia Polytechnic Institute 131
Virginia State Library 131
Visual Dictionary CD-ROM 85
VLS Inc. 123
VoxCard 126
Voyager 125

Wall Street Journal 87, 90, 99
Wang Inc. 121
Ward's Business Directory 90, 105
WBLA Inc. 129
West Publishing Co. 121
Western Library Network (WLN) 77
WESTLAW database 121
Who's Who in Finance and Industry 104
Wild card 6, 70, 113
Wilson 92, 94-96
WILSONDISC line 94-95
Windows/On the World software 130-131
WordStar 104
Work assignments 50-51
Workstation location 48
World Almanac and Book of Facts 85
Worldscope 107
Wright Investors' Service 106
Write rates 59

Year Book Medical Publishers 93
Your Marketing Consultant 109

Zip + 4 Directory 115, 123